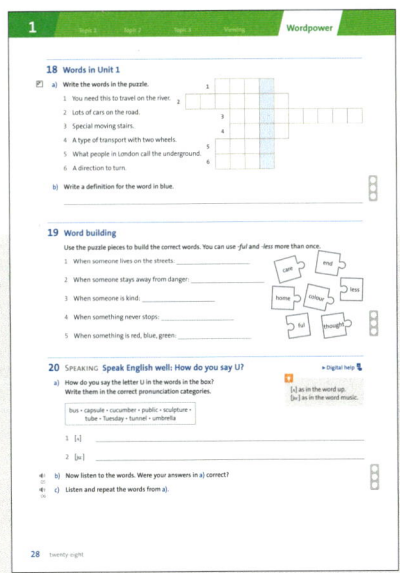

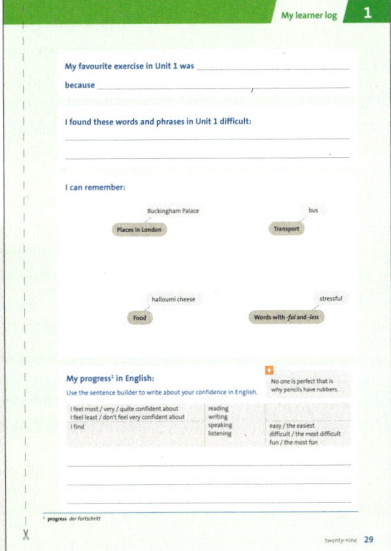

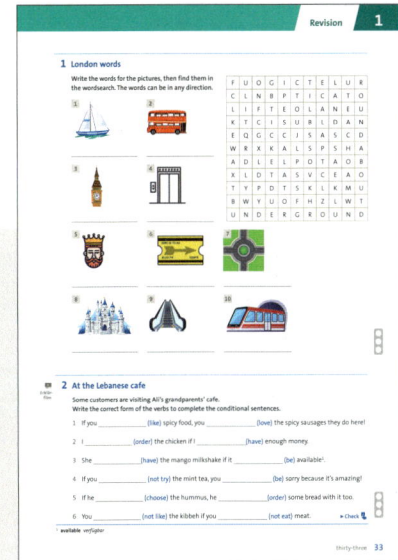

Wordpower

Auf dieser Seite findest du Übungen zu den Vokabeln der jeweiligen Units und kannst dein gesprochenes Englisch verbessern.

My learner log

Hier kannst du auf die Unit zurückblicken und deinen Lernstand festhalten.

Revision

Halte auf diesen Seiten inne und wiederhole, was du in den vorherigen Units gelernt hast.

Diese Verweise führen dich in die *Diff bank* am Ende der Unit

▶ More help	▶ Early finisher	▶ Challenge
Hilfen zu den Aufgaben	weitere Übungen	weitere Übungen mit höherem Schwierigkeitsgrad

Dein Buch findest du auch in der Cornelsen Lernen App

Siehst du eines dieser Symbole in deinem Workbook, kannst du in deiner App …

🔊 ▶️ Erklär-film	▶ Digital help	▶ Check
alle Hörtexte und Videos zu deinem Arbeitsheft aufrufen.	auf Ideen und Hilfen zugreifen.	deine Antworten eigenständig überprüfen.

lighthouse 3

Workbook Lehrkräftefassung

Im Auftrag des Verlages erarbeitet von
Zoe Thorne, Royston

In Zusammenarbeit mit der Englischredaktion
Klaus Unger (Projektleitung),
Lisa Ahmadi (verantwortliche Redakteurin), Chiara Castellano,
Michael Dunkel, Christine House, Melina Frick, Karin Wedepohl

Beratende Mitwirkung
Anke Barth, Plauen; Armin Düpmeier, Warendorf; Lara Jano, Rottweil
und Stefan Herzberg, Berlin *(Check-up)*; Sonja Mahne, Basel
(My learner log); Jimmy Miller, Berlin *(Check-up)*

Medienmanagement
Silke Kirchhoff

Illustrationen
Yaroslav Schwarzstein, Hannover

Fotos
Anja Poehlmann, Brighton
Chocolate Films, London

Umschlaggestaltung
Rosendahl, Berlin

Layoutkonzept
Klein & Halm, Berlin

Layout und technische Umsetzung
PER MEDIEN & MARKETING GmbH, Braunschweig

www.cornelsen.de

Druck: Athesiadruck GmbH

1. Auflage, 1. Druck 2024
Workbook 3
ISBN 978-3-06-036544-9

1. Auflage, 1. Druck 2024
Workbook 3 Lehrkräftefassung
ISBN 978-3-06-036545-6

Passend zum Workbook:
Sprechen, Aussprache, Wortschatz und Grammatik digital üben
mit der mobilen App ChatClass. Erhältlich auch als PrintPlus-Lizenz
bei Nutzung des Arbeitsheftes.

PEFC-zertifiziert
Dieses Produkt
stammt aus
nachhaltig
bewirtschafteten
Wäldern und
kontrollierten Quellen

lighthouse 3

Workbook Lehrkräftefassung

 Audios online verfügbar unter
go.cornelsen.de

Code: mokuta

 Dein Workbook findest du auch in der **Cornelsen Lernen App**.

Siehst du eines dieser Symbole in deinem Workbook, findest du in der App …

🔊 alle **Audios**

▶️ alle **Videos** und **Erklärfilme**

↩️ **Hilfen** und **Lösungen** zu ausgewählten Aufgaben

Quellenverzeichnis

Titelbild
Cornelsen/li.: Shutterstock.com/Ron Ellis/courtesy of Transport for London; Personen: Chocolate Films; Hintergrund re.: stock.adobe.com/anatoliycherkas

Illustrationen
Cornelsen/Yaroslav Schwarzstein: S. 23/m., S. 25/o. r., S. 32/m. r., S. 38/m., S. 38/m. l., S. 38/m. r., S. 38/u. l., S. 38/u. m., S. 38/u. r., S. 40/o. r., S. 47/m., S. 47/m. l., S. 47/m. r., S. 47/o. m., S. 47/u. l., S. 47/u. m., S. 47/u. r., S. 50/m., S. 52/o. r., S. 53/m., S. 53/m. l., S. 53/m. r., S. 53/u. l., S. 53/u. m., S. 53/u. r., S. 57/m., S. 58/m., S. 58/m. l., S. 58/m. r., S. 58/u. l., S. 58/u. m., S. 58/u. r., S. 63/m., S. 63/m. l., S. 63/m. r., S. 63/u. l., S. 63/u. m., S. 63/u. r., S. 70/u. l., S. 70/u. m., S. 70/u. r., S. 71/m., S. 71/m. l., S. 71/o. l., S. 71/o. m., S. 74/m., S. 74/m. l., S. 74/m. r., S. 79/o. l., S. 79/o. m., S. 79/o. r., S. 81/o. m., S. 89/m., S. 91/m., S. 91/m. l., S. 91/u. l.

Abbildungen
S. 3/u. l.: Cornelsen/Inhouse/Anne Weingarten; **S. 5**/m. l.: Shutterstock.com/Fotimageon; **S. 5**/m.: stock.adobe.com/Kaspars; **S. 5**/o. l.: Shutterstock.com/S-F; **S. 5**/u. l.: Shutterstock.com/John McGreevy; **S. 5**/u. l.: stock.adobe.com/Tomas Marek; **S. 7**/m.: stock.adobe.com/Prostock-studio; **S. 7**/m. l.: Imago Stock & People GmbH/Design Pics; **S. 7**/m. r.: stock.adobe.com/Pixel-Shot; **S. 7**/o. l.: stock.adobe.com/kelvn; **S. 7**/o. m.: Imago Stock & People GmbH/Design Pics; **S. 7**/o. r.: Imago Stock & People GmbH/Zoonar; **S. 7**/u. r.: stock.adobe.com/jelenaaloskina; **S. 8**/o. l.: Imago Stock & People GmbH/Tom Mackie/Avalon.red; **S. 8**/o. m.: Imago Stock & People GmbH/Zoonar; **S. 8**/o. r.: Imago Stock & People GmbH/imago images/agefotostock/BuildPix/Photoshot; **S. 9**/u. r.: Cornelsen/Anja Poehlmann; **S. 10**/m. r.: Cornelsen/Anja Poehlmann; **S. 10**/m. r.: Shutterstock.com/Tsekhmister; **S. 11**/o. r.: Cornelsen/Anja Poehlmann; **S. 12**/o. l., o. r.: Cornelsen/Anja Poehlmann; **S. 14**/m. r.: stock.adobe.com/Mix and Match Studio; **S. 14**/m. r.: stock.adobe.com/stockyimages; **S. 16**/u. r.: stock.adobe.com/Eli Bolyarska; **S. 21**/m.: stock.adobe.com/marcorubino; **S. 21**/m. l.: stock.adobe.com/elena; **S. 21**/m. r.: Imago Stock & People GmbH/agefotostock/claudiodivizi; **S. 21**/o. l.: Shutterstock.com/QQ7; **S. 21**/o. m.: stock.adobe.com/Bonsai Multimedia/chbaum; **S. 21**/o. r.: mauritius images/alamy stock photo/Mickey Lee; **S. 21**/u. r.: stock.adobe.com/Andrew Barker; **S. 22**/m. r.: Imago Stock & People GmbH/imagebroker/Mara Brandl; **S. 22**/o. r.: Cornelsen/Chocolate Films; **S. 24**/u. m.: Shutterstock.com/Pixel-Shot; **S. 25**/m. r.: stock.adobe.com/Wigandt; **S. 26**/u. r.: Imago Stock & People GmbH/Addictive Stock/David Fuentes; **S. 27**/u. r.: Digital Learning Ass. Ltd.; **S. 28**/m. r.: stock.adobe.com/binik; **S. 30**/u. r.: stock.adobe.com/yurolaitsalbert; **S. 31**/m. l.: Shutterstock.com/Carboxylase; **S. 31**/m. l.: stock.adobe.com/inspiring.team; **S. 31**/m. r.: Imago Stock & People GmbH/imagebroker/Mara Brandl; **S. 31**/o. l.: Shutterstock.com/Carboxylase; **S. 31**/o. l., o. m.: Shutterstock.com/Carboxylase; **S. 33**/m.: mauritius images/Maximilian Laschon/Alamy Stock Photos; **S. 33**/m.: mauritius images/YAY Media AS/Alamy Stock Photos; **S. 33**/m.: Shutterstock.com/Boyko.Pictures; **S. 33**/m. l.: stock.adobe.com/mr_marcom; **S. 33**/m. l.: stock.adobe.com/Zaharia Levy; **S. 33**/m. r.: Shutterstock.com/Boyko.Pictures; **S. 33**/o. l.: mauritius images/Tomacco/Alamy Stock Photos; **S. 33**/o. l.: stock.adobe.com/topvectors; **S. 33**/o. m.: mauritius images/Tomacco/Alamy Stock Photos; **S. 33**/o. m.: Shutterstock.com/Premiumvectors; **S. 34**/u. m.: Cornelsen/Chocolate Films; **S. 35**/m.: mauritius images/Cavan Images; **S. 35**/m. l.: Imago Stock & People GmbH/Addictive Stock/Franci Leoncio; **S. 35**/m. r.: Imago Stock & People GmbH/Addictive Stock/CienXCien Studio; **S. 36**/m. r.: Shutterstock.com/HollyHarry; **S. 40**/u. r.: Imago Stock & People GmbH/Addictive Stock/Franci Leoncio; **S. 41**/o. r.: Imago Sportfotodienst GmbH/PA Images; **S. 42**/m.: stock.adobe.com/guas; **S. 43**/m. r.: Cornelsen/Chocolate Films; **S. 44**/u. r.: stock.adobe.com/contrastwerkstatt; **S. 45**/u. l.: stock.adobe.com/Icons-Studio; **S. 49**/m. r.: Cornelsen/Chocolate Films; **S. 51**/u. m.: Shutterstock.com/Panda Vector; **S. 55**/m. r.: Imago Stock & People GmbH/imago/Westend61; **S. 56**/o. r.: stock.adobe.com/Maridav; **S. 58**/o. r.: Imago Stock & People GmbH/Wirestock; **S. 59**/m.: Digital Learning Ass. Ltd.; **S. 59**/m. l.: Digital Learning Ass. Ltd.; **S. 59**/m. r.: Digital Learning Ass. Ltd.; **S. 64**/m. l.: Shutterstock.com/Ground Picture; **S. 65**/u. r.: Imago Stock & People GmbH/Shotshop; **S. 66**/m. r.: stock.adobe.com/David Pimborough; **S. 67**/m. l.: Imago Stock & People GmbH; **S. 67**/m. l.: mauritius images/TinasDreamworld/Alamy Stock Photos; **S. 67**/m. l.: stock.adobe.com/mtrommer; **S. 67**/m. l.: stock.adobe.com/tinasdreamworld; **S. 67**/o. l.: stock.adobe.com/dudlajzov; **S. 68**/o. r.: stock.adobe.com/New Africa; **S. 69**/o. r.: Imago Stock & People GmbH/imago images/MASKOT; **S. 70**/o. r.: Depositphotos/Abhishek Rastogi; **S. 70**/o. r.: stock.adobe.com/Bhaven; **S. 72**/m. l.: Shutterstock.com/Ebtikar; **S. 72**/m. l.: stock.adobe.com/Sangiao_Photography; **S. 72**/o. l.: Depositphotos/XAVIER LORENZO; **S. 73**/m. r.: Shutterstock.com/AYO Production; **S. 75**/u. l.: Shutterstock.com/Maksim Denisenko; **S. 78**/u. r.: Cornelsen/Chocolate Films; **S. 79**/m. r.: Jeff Koterba, Cagle Cartoons via CartoonStock.com; **S. 81**/u. r.: Cornelsen/Chocolate Films; **S. 82**/m. r.: Imago Stock & People GmbH/robertharding; **S. 83**/o. r.: stock.adobe.com/worldwide_stock; **S. 84**/m. r.: Shutterstock.com/Ariya J; **S. 84**/o. r.: stock.adobe.com/Ruth P. Peterkin; **S. 90**/m. r.: Imago Stock & People GmbH/Loop Images/Highwaystarz.

Hello!
Where we're from

Unit 1
London: City life

Revision 1

Unit 2
Manchester: Who we are

Revision 2

Unit 3
Scotland: Adventure

Revision 3

Unit 4
Wales: Digital life

Revision 4

Unit 5
Two Irelands: Together

Partner pages

Die Check-up-Seiten können zur Ermittlung der Lernausgangslage genutzt werden.

1 Opposites

Match the adjectives 1–6 with their opposites a–g.
There's one opposite that you don't need.

a boring	b late	c lazy	d light	e nervous	f scary	g slow

1 fast — *g*   2 interesting — *a*   3 dark — *d*

4 confident — *e*   5 hard-working — *c*   6 early — *b*   ▶ Check ____ / 6

2 Find the verb

Write a verb that can fit with each group of words.

1 *play* _____ tennis / computer games / the guitar

2 *go* _____ to the cinema / into town / to the beach / on holiday / shopping

3 *listen* _____ to music / to the teacher / to a speech

4 *watch* _____ TV / a film / a video / a football match

5 *do* _____ your homework / yoga / the dishes / a puzzle

6 *get* _____ dressed / married / up / pocket money   ▶ Check ____ / 6

3 Odd word out

Which word doesn't fit? Write why.
You get one point for each correct odd word out and one point for each correct explanation.

1 excited   kind   rude   patient

Rude doesn't fit because it's a negative adjective/word.

2 swimming   reading   trampolining   football

Reading doesn't fit because it's not a sport.

3 friend   brother   cousin   stepmother

Friend doesn't fit because it's not a family member.

4 chicken   sausage   ham   potato

Potato doesn't fit because it's not a type of meat / it's a vegetable.

5 maths   French   geography   classroom

Classroom doesn't fit because it's not a subject / it's a room.

6 bed   shower   wardrobe   chair

Shower doesn't fit because it's not in the bedroom.

▶ Check ____ / 12

🔊 01

4 Chloe's morning

Listen to Lily's sister Chloe talking about her mornings and complete the clocks.

07:30

07:45

08:00

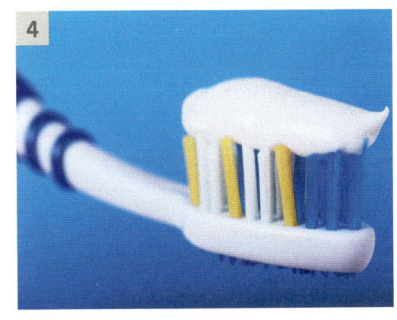

08:20

08:25

08:45

▶ Check 🔧 _____ / 6

🔊 02

5 Meeting Dario

a) Listen to the conversation. What kind of conversation is it?

It's an interview for a job.

b) Listen again and circle the correct answers.

1 Dario wants to be a shop assistant / babysitter / cleaner.

2 Dario has never done this job before / has done this job a lot.

3 Dario is 13 / 14 / 15 years old.

4 Dario is never reliable / hard-working / late.

5 Dario maybe wants to be a teacher / captain / cricket player one day.

6 Dario doesn't get the job / doesn't want the job / gets the job.

▶ Check 🔧 _____ / 7

6 Which home?

Match the photos (A–C) to the adverts (1–3). Write the correct letter in the box.

1

FOR SALE[1]: Modern flat with two bedrooms, one bathroom and a balcony on the fourth floor in the town centre.
B

2

FOR SALE: Small, quiet house with a garden in the country. Ground floor only.
C

3

FOR SALE: Big, traditional house with two floors and four bedrooms. Small garden with trees and flowers.
A

► Check _____ / 3

7 Our chores

Read the three messages and the seven sentences.
Write if each sentence is about PizzaFan55 (P), SurferGirl (S) or BookWorm42 (B).

> **PizzaFan55**   *What chores do you have to do, everyone? I think my dad is so mean because I have to help SO much at home. I have to set the table for dinner every night AND then empty the dishwasher. I also have to take out the rubbish once a week. It's not fair!*

> **SurferGirl**   *Oh, that's a lot! I'm lucky – I don't have to do many chores. I have to tidy my room sometimes, of course, and I have to babysit my little sister once a month. But that's it! I'm happy I don't have to take out the rubbish or clean the bathroom – yuck!*

> **BookWorm42**   *I don't have to do any chores if I don't want to, but I can if I want to earn pocket money. My parents give me money when I help at home. For example, when I vacuum the floors, I get £3. I think it's a great idea and sometimes I do lots of chores if I'm saving up for something! That way, everyone is happy.*

1 This person isn't happy with their situation.   P

2 This person doesn't have to help at home.   B

3 This person has to do a chore every day.   P

4 This person has to look after someone.   S

5 This person has to tidy their room.   S

6 This person sometimes does extra chores.   B

7 This person has to take out the rubbish.   P

► Check _____ / 7

[1] **for sale** *zu verkaufen*

8 Finn's holiday

Read Finn's email to Sunita and say if the sentences are true (T) or false (F).

to	Sunita
from	Finn

Hey Sunita

How are you? Did you have a nice holiday?

We've just got back from holiday. Normally, we go to an island in the north of Germany called Usedom, and we stay in a holiday house by the beach there. It's fun but the weather can be cold and windy, which isn't so good!

So it was great that we did something a bit different this year. We went to Turkey to visit my dad's family, and we stayed with my aunt and uncle in Istanbul. It's an amazing city – you'd love it! I went there once when I was really little, but I didn't remember it, of course.

It's a bit different to most cities because it's actually on two continents[1]. My aunt and uncle live on the east side of the river, in Asia, but we often took the ferry over to the west side, so we could go sightseeing[2] in Europe! We visited lots of beautiful mosques and the biggest market in the world! I bought a present for my friend Suri, but we didn't buy any spices because my aunt prefers to get those in the market near her house instead.

It was Ramadan while we were there, so we didn't eat or drink during the day. But most evenings, we went to a big park called Sultanahmet Square, where lots of people had picnics and music to celebrate the end of the fast. People sold all kinds of food and drink, but my favourite was the apple tea!

Did you do anything fun during the holidays? It was your first holiday together with Ben and Willow too, right?

Write to me soon and tell me everything!

Finn

1 Finn went to the island of Usedom this year.   F

2 He doesn't like the weather on his normal holiday.   T

3 He stayed in a holiday home in Turkey.   F

4 It was his first time in Istanbul.   F

5 He sometimes went to the other side of the city by boat.   T

6 He bought spices for his friend in the big market.   F

7 He ate evening meals outside with other people.   T

8 He really liked a hot drink.   T

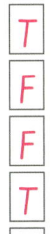

▶ Check ⬇ ____ / 8

---

1 **continent** *der Kontinent*   2 **sightseeing** *die Besichtigung von Sehenswürdigkeiten*

9 Coding Robbie

a) Sunita is coding her robot Robbie. Complete the rules to make the simple past tense for regular verbs in English.

```
1  For most verbs, add  ed .
```
! Irregular verbs have a special form.

```
2  If the verb ends in -e, add  d .

3  If the verb ends in a consonant and -y, change the -y to  ie .
```
/3

b) Complete the text with the verbs in the simple past. Remember that some verbs are irregular!

Yesterday, there (1) _was_ (be) a new pet in Sunita's home –

Meera (2) _brought_ (bring) home a sick kitten! Sunita

(3) _liked_ (like) the kitten and she (4) _played_ (play)

with it all afternoon. She (5) _gave_ (give) it some milk and the

kitten (6) _slept_ (sleep) next to her. But it (7) _got up_

(get up) a lot in the night and (8) _tried_ (try) to jump on all the beds, so they

(9) _were_ (be) all very tired the next day! And they (10) _weren't_ (not be)

/10

happy!

c) Sunita asked Robbie some questions to test her code. Look at the highlighted verbs in Robbie's answers. Use them to complete the questions in the simple past.

1 What _did_ you _eat_ for breakfast this morning?

   – I'm a robot, so I didn't eat any breakfast!

2 What _did_ you _help_ me with yesterday?

   – I helped you with your homework.

3 Where _did_ the kitten _sleep_ last night?

   – It slept in your bed.

4 Who _sent_ me a message today? – Finn sent you a message.

5 What _was_ the weather like yesterday? – It was cold but sunny.

6 _Did_ you _take_ the chocolate in my room? – No, Nish took it, not me!

/6

▶ Check 🔽 _____ / 19

10 An interview with Jodie

Jodie is one of the head students at Varndean School. Complete the interview with verbs from the box in the simple present.

> be (x4) • not dance • do (x2) • go • have • love • make • meet • sing • want • watch

Raj Hi Jodie! What year *are* _____ (1) you in?

Jodie I *'m* _____ (2) in Year 11.

Raj What *'s* _____ (3) your favourite subject and why?

Jodie I *love* _____ (4) design and technology because the teacher *is* _____ (5) nice. Also, my dad *has* _____ (6) a garage and I *want* _____ (7) to be a mechanic like him one day.

Raj What do you *do* _____ (8) in your free time?

Jodie Sometimes I *go* _____ (9) to the gym[1] or I *sing* _____ (10) in the school choir[2]. Or I *meet* _____ (11) my friends and we all sit and *watch* _____ (12) funny videos together. My best friend *does* _____ (13) street dance every week, so she often *makes* _____ (14) her own cool dance videos. But not me – I *don't dance* _____ (15) ever!

▶ Check ⬇ _____ / 15

11 Weather forecast

Look at the weather forecast. Write sentences using the will-future for each picture.

It'll be sunny in the north. / There will be sun in the north.

It'll be rainy / rain in the west. / There will be rain in the west.

It'll be windy in the south. / There will be wind in the south.

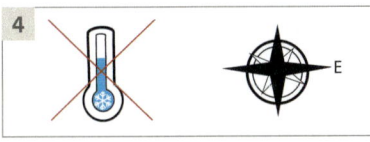

It won't be cold in the east.

It'll be snowy / snow in the mountains.

It won't rain / be rainy at the beach.

▶ Check ⬇ _____ / 6

---

[1] **gym** *das Fitnessstudio*   [2] **school choir** *der Schulchor*

👥 12 An invitation

Zane is inviting Lily to a party. Partner A is Zane and Partner B is Lily. Act the conversation with a partner. Use the pictures to help you. You get one point for every correct line of the dialogue.

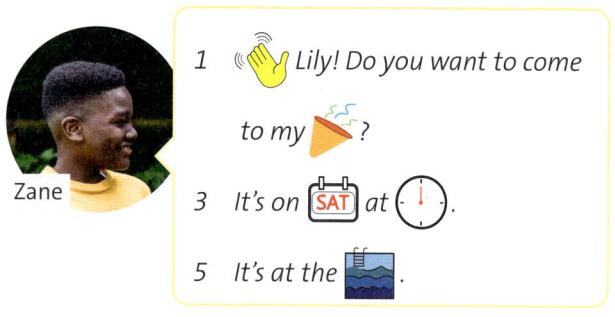

▶ Check 🔽 _____ / 3

13 My school life

a) Use the information below to give a one-minute talk about your school life. Make notes in your exercise book. You can record your talk.

Remember to	Points
– name your two favourite places in school.	___ / 2
– describe the two places.	___ / 2
– use adjectives in your descriptions of the places in school.	___ / 1
– name two subjects you like.	___ / 2
– explain why you like those two subjects.	___ / 2
– name one subject you don't like.	___ / 1
– explain why you don't like that subject.	___ / 1
– use the simple present to talk about the places at school and the subjects.	___ / 1
– say what you did at school yesterday.	___ / 1
– use the simple past to talk about what you did at school yesterday.	___ / 1
– speak slowly.	___ / 1
– speak clearly.	___ / 1

👥 b) Present your talk to a partner or give them your recording. Your partner gives feedback in the table in a).

▶ Check 🔽 _____ / 16

14 My favourite character

a) Use the information below to write a description of your favourite character from a book, film, series or game. First make notes.

(Harry Potter, eleven years old, black hair, round glasses, old clothes, uniform, student, magic, brave and adventurous, his friends)

Remember to	Points
– say three things about the character (age, where they live, what they do, …).	____ / 3
– use adjectives to describe what the character looks like.	____ / 1
– describe what the character wears.	____ / 1
– use adjectives to describe the character's personality.	____ / 1
– say why you like that character.	____ / 1
– use the simple present.	____ / 1
– use the correct word order.	____ / 1
– use the correct spelling.	____ / 1

b) Now write your text. Write about 70–80 words.

(Harry Potter is my favourite character! He has messy black hair and round glasses. Harry wears old clothes from his cousin or his school uniform because he's a student at a magical school called Hogwarts. In the first book he is eleven years old and finds out that he can use magic! He's brave and adventurous. He fights the bad guy Voldemort and is a great friend to Ron and Hermione. It's fun to read about his magical adventures!)

c) Give your text to a partner. Your partner reads the text and gives feedback in the table in a).

► Check 🔖 ____ / 10

15 A lost pet

Read the poster for a lost pet and explain it in German. Give yourself a point for each piece of information (what happened, description, what the pet does, what you should do).

Can you help? Our dog **Bingo** ran away yesterday. He is quite big but very friendly, and he's **black and white**. He loves running after a ball and he will come to you if you call him. If you see him, please text this number!

07700 900426

Gestern ist ein großer, schwarz–weißer und lieber Hund namens Bingo entlaufen. Er spielt gerne mit dem Ball und hört auf seinen Namen. Falls ihn jemand sieht, dann bitte unter der angegebenen Nummer melden.

▶ Check ⬇ _____ / 4

16 In the restaurant

You are in a restaurant in Brighton with your grandmother, who doesn't speak English.
Write what you will say to each person below.

Waiter Hello, what would you like to order?

YOU *Er möchte deine Bestellung aufnehmen.* (1 point)

Grandma Kannst du ihn fragen, was es für vegetarisches Essen gibt?

YOU *What vegetarian food do you have?* (1 point)

Waiter We have a pizza with cheese and tomato or a veggie burger with chips.

YOU *Es gibt Pizza mit Käse und Tomaten oder einen Veggieburger mit Pommes.* (1 point)

Grandma Dann nehme ich den Veggieburger aber mit Salat statt Pommes, bitte.

YOU *She'll have the veggie burger, but with a salad and not chips, please.* (1 point)

Waiter Yes, and what would you like to drink?

YOU *Und was magst du trinken?* (1 point)

Grandma Ein Glas Mineralwasser, bitte.

YOU *She would like sparkling water, please.* (1 point)

Waiter Of course. And how about your order?

▶ Check ⬇ _____ / 6

Evaluating[1] my skills

Complete the table with your points from pages 6–14. Then colour the traffic lights.

Skill	Points			Evaluation		Übungsmaterial
Vocabulary	**1** [ ] + **2** [ ] + **3** [ ] = total [ ]			19–24 = green / 13–18 = orange / 12 or under = red	⚫⚫⚫	Check-up: Vocabulary 1 / Check-up: Vocabulary 2 / Check-up: Vocabulary 3 / Check-up: Vocabulary 4
Listening	**4** [ ] + **5** [ ] = total [ ]			11–13 = green / 7–10 = orange / 6 or under = red	⚫⚫⚫	Check-up: Listening 1 / Check-up: Listening 2 / Check-up: Listening 3 / Check-up: Listening 4
Reading	**6** [ ] + **7** [ ] + **8** [ ] = total [ ]			15–18 = green / 10–14 = orange / 9 or under = red	⚫⚫⚫	Check-up: Reading 1 / Check-up: Reading 2 / Check-up: Reading 3 / Check-up: Reading 4 / Check-up: Reading 5
Grammar	**9** [ ] + **10** [ ] + **11** [ ] = total [ ]			31–40 = green / 21–30 = orange / 20 or under = red	⚫⚫⚫	Check-up: Grammar 1 / Check-up: Grammar 2 / Check-up: Grammar 3 / Check-up: Grammar 4 / Check-up: Grammar 5 / Check-up: Grammar 6
Speaking	**12** [ ] + **13** [ ] = total [ ]			15–19 = green / 10–14 = orange / 9 or under = red	⚫⚫⚫	Check-up: Speaking 1 / Check-up: Speaking 2 / Check-up: Speaking 3
Writing	**14** [ ]			9–10 = green / 6–8 = orange / 5 or under = red	⚫⚫⚫	Check-up: Writing 1 / Check-up: Writing 2 / Check-up: Writing 3
Mediation	**15** [ ] + **16** [ ] = total [ ]			9–10 = green / 6–8 = orange / 5 or under = red	⚫⚫⚫	Check-up: Mediation 1 / Check-up: Mediation 2

Nachdem die Lernausgangslage mit dem *Check-up* ermittelt wurde, können die Schülerinnen und Schüler individuell mit dem Übungsmaterial gefördert und gefordert werden. Das Übungsmaterial besteht aus Kopiervorlagen auf bis zu vier Niveaustufen:

☑ Förder-Niveau   ☒ mittleres Niveau

☑ einfaches Niveau   ☒ hohes/forderndes Niveau

Die Rückseiten der Kopiervorlagen sind zur Selbstkontrolle mit den Lösungen versehen. Für *Speaking*- und *Writing*-Aufgaben, die den Erfahrungshorizont der Schülerinnen und Schüler einbeziehen und somit sehr individuell gelöst werden, gibt es zum Teil Musterlösungen. Hier sind aber auch Sie als Feedback-Instanz gefragt.

Zusammengestellt wurde dieses Übungsmaterial aus dem Material Extra-Differenzierung zu *Lighthouse Band 1* und 2. Sie finden die Kopiervorlagen im *Unterrichtsmanager Plus* zu Band 3 von *Lighthouse*.

---

[1] **(to) evaluate sth.** *etw. beurteilen, etw. einschätzen*

Hello!
Where we're from

1 READING Places in the book

▶ Digital help   ▶ SB, p. 13

Read the photo descriptions and find the photos in your book. Write the page number for each one.

1   This is a photo of Conwy Castle in North Wales. The sky is blue and in the foreground there's a white bridge over the river. (Hello!-Unit) *page 13*

2   This is a photo of St James's Park in the middle of London. In the foreground, there's a large lake with four white birds near it. (Unit 1) *page 20*

3   This is a photo of Manchester in the north-west of England. It's a small photo, but you can see a park, and lots of tall buildings in the background. (Unit 2) *page 45*

4   This is a photo of the high street in Edinburgh, the capital of Scotland. You can see a tall church[1] and, on the right of the picture, some red phone boxes. (Unit 3) *page 75*

5   This is a photo of a beach in Wales. On the left of the picture, you can see two people and some donkeys. (Unit 4) *page 106*

6   This is a photo of the Giant's Causeway near Belfast in Northern Ireland. There are lots of big rocks near the sea and in the background, there's an orange sun. (Unit 5) *page 138*

2 WRITING A photo description

▶ SB, p. 13

Look at the photo of another place in the UK, Inverness, and write a description as in exercise 1. Use the words and phrases in exercise 1 to help you.

(This is a photo of Inverness. In the foreground, there's a bridge over the river. There are people on the bridge. In the background, you can see two big churches. In front of the church on the left there's a small park. The sky is grey and cloudy. / ...)

---

[1] **church** *die Kirche*

3 READING More UK cities

▶ SB, p.13

Read the descriptions and write the cities on the map of the UK.

1   Aberdeen is a city in the north-east of Scotland.

2   Brighton is a city on the south coast[1] of England, just south of London.

3   Derry (sometimes called Londonderry) is a city in the north-west of Northern Ireland.

4   Newcastle is a city in the north of England, near the border with Scotland.

5   Norwich is a city in the east of England.

6   Plymouth is a city on the south-west coast of England.

7   Swansea is a city on the south coast of Wales, near Cardiff.

8   York is a city in the north-east of England. It's to the south of Newcastle.

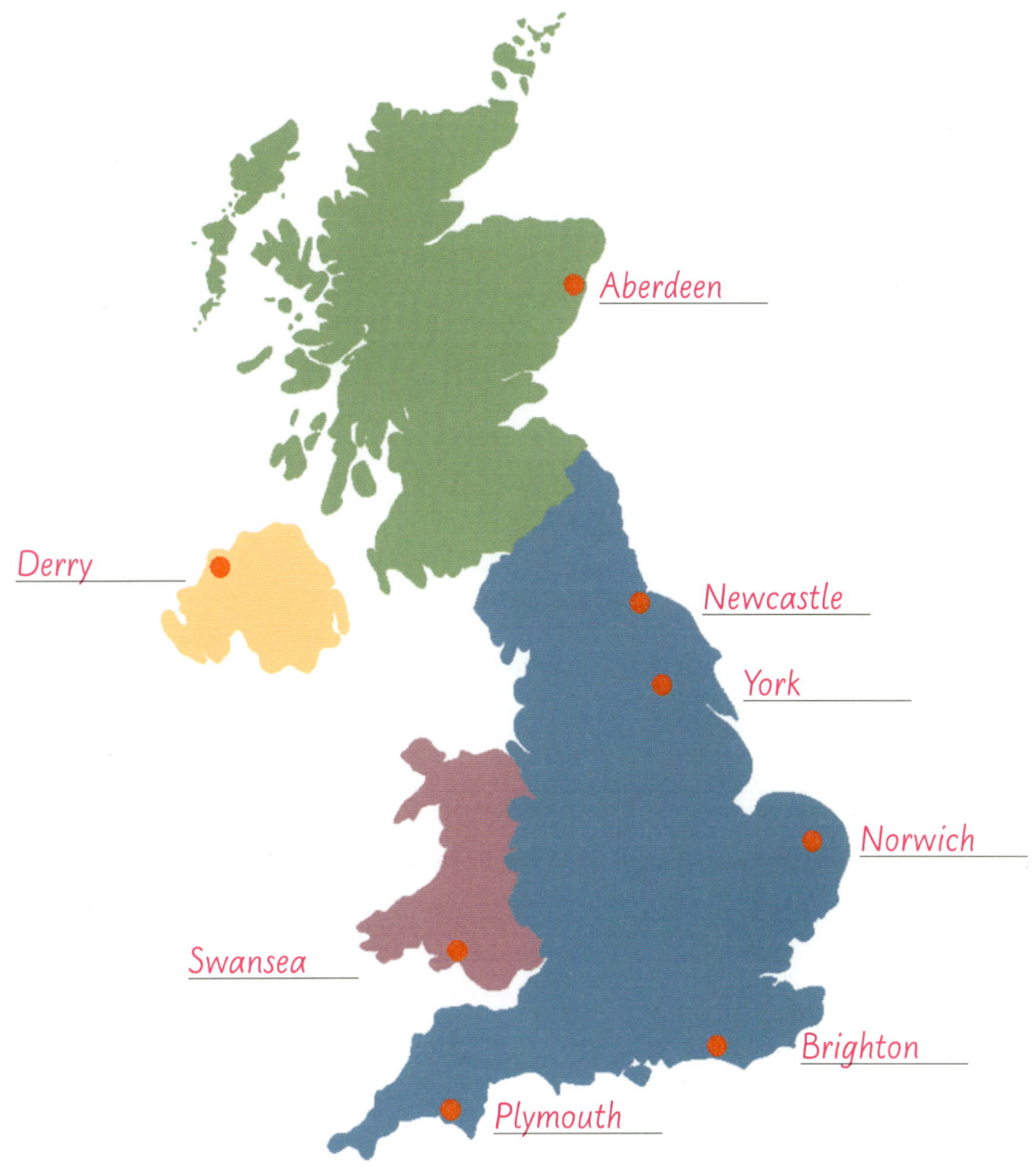

[1] **coast** *die Küste*

Unit 1
London: City life

1 London sights

► SB, p. 15

a) Write the words in the puzzle. All the words are on pages 14–15 of your book.

1 The Leake Street ...

2 You can see musicians by the river here. *(two words)*

3 You can buy things to eat outside here. *(two words)*

4 A tall part of a building.

5 A type of art, like 6.

6 The Orbit ...

7 A place where anyone can draw. *(two words)*

8 The London Eye is a ... *(two words)*

9 A famous clock. *(two words)*

Crossword:
1 Down: TUNNELS
2 Down: SOUTHBANK
3 Down: FOODSTALL
4 Across: TOWER
5 Down: SCULPTURE
6 Across: SLIDE
7 Across: GRAFFITIWALL
8 Across: BIGWHEEL
9 Across: BIGBEN

b) How many London sights can you remember? Write them below, then **highlight** the ones you most want to visit.

Big Ben, Camden Market, Houses of Parliament, Leake Street Tunnel,

London Eye, Orbit Slide, South Bank.

I can **understand and share information about London.**

2 On the tube

► SB, p. 17

Look at the underground ticket and choose the correct words from the box.

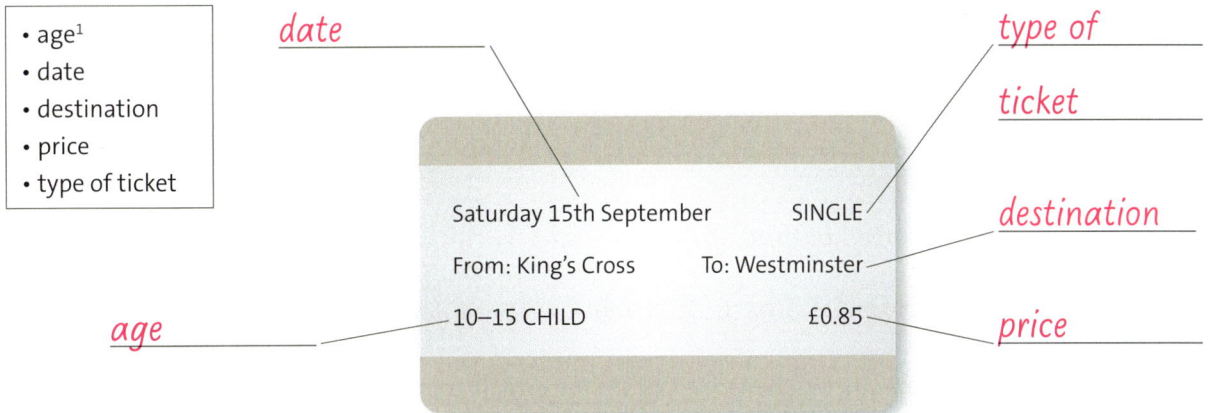

- age[1]
- date
- destination
- price
- type of ticket

date

type of ticket

destination

age

Saturday 15th September   SINGLE

From: King's Cross   To: Westminster

10–15 CHILD   £0.85

price

3 READING Journey puzzle

► SB, p. 17

a) Ali, Lily and Pearl are going to different places in London on Saturday.
    Read the sentences and complete the table with the words from the three boxes.

Destination:
King's Cross
Houses of Parliament
Orbit Slide

Transport:
bus
city bike
underground

Price:
85p
£1.65
free

1   Pearl will go to a train station, but she won't take the tube.

2   Ali will cycle, but his journey will be the most expensive.

3   Lily won't ride on a slide, but she will take the tube.

4   Pearl's journey won't cost anything.

	Destination	Transport	Price
Ali	*Orbit Slide*	*city bike*	*£1.65*
Lily	*Houses of Parliament*	*underground*	*85p*
Pearl	*King's Cross*	*bus*	*free*

b) Look at the table again. Who will use the ticket in exercise 2?

Lily will use the ticket.

---

[1] **age** *das Alter*

4   MEDIATION   Buying a ticket

▶ SB, p. 17

Help Suzanne, a German tourist, buy a ticket in London. Write what you will say to each person below.

Mo   Hello, can I help you?

Suzanne   Kannst du ihn nach dem besten Ticket zur Oxford Street fragen?

You   *Can you tell me the best ticket to Oxford Street, please?*

Mo   Of course. Do you need a single or return?

You   *Brauchen Sie eine Einzelfahrkarte oder eine Rückfahrkarte?*

Suzanne   Ich bin mir nicht sicher. Ich möchte heute auch andere Orte in London besuchen.

You   *She's not sure. She also wants to visit other places in London today.*

Mo   Oh, in that case, it's cheapest to get a Travelcard. You can use it all day, on buses and the tube.

You   *Am günstigsten ist es, eine sogenannte Travelcard zu kaufen.*

          Das ist eine Tageskarte für Bus und U-Bahn.

Suzanne   Wunderbar! Wieviel kostet die Tageskarte? Kann ich mit Karte bezahlen?

You   *How much is it and can she pay by card?*

Mo   Sure, no problem. It's £15.20.

You   *Ja, Sie können mit Karte bezahlen und sie kostet £15,20.*

5   READING   An underground poem

▶ SB, p. 17

There are poems on the underground to help people remember the rules.
Read the poem and (circle) the correct answers.

1 The poem is about (being polite) / buying a ticket.

2 People who want to move on the escalators should go to the (left) / right.

3 It's important to move quickly / (safely) in the underground station.

4 You should get on the train quickly / (give people space).

5 The last line means you should (be careful when you get on the train) / not use your phone.

> Lots of people use the tube
> So please remember, don't be rude
> On escalators, day and night
> Walk on the left, stand on the right
> Always walk and never run
> Then there'll be space for everyone
> When the train arrives, stand back
> And when it's your turn, mind the gap!

▶ Challenge 1, p. 31

I can **talk about transport in London.**

6 LISTENING **A tour of London**

► SB, p. 18

a) Listen to the tour guide. What kind of tour is it? (Circle) the correct answer.

    A   Music Tour   (B)   Ghost Tour   C   Segway Tour

b) Listen again and tick (✓) the places that the people see on the tour.

⬜ Buckingham Palace   ☑ Houses of Parliament   ☑ London Dungeon

⬜ London Eye   ☑ Shakespeare's Globe Theatre   ☑ Tower of London

7 WRITING **My dream tour of London**

► Digital help 🔖   ► SB, p. 18

Complete the sentences about your dream tour of London.
Write one sentence about another place you want to see and why.

On my dream tour of London, I want to travel by
(Segway / bike / taxi / ...) .

I want to visit *(Buckingham Palace)*

because *(the King lives there)*

_____

and I also want to see *(the Tower of London)*

because *(it's scary and I like ghosts)* .

(I want to visit the Orbis Slide because the sculpture looks cool and I like fast

rides.)

Erklär-film

8 LANGUAGE **What will Ali do?**   ▶ SB, p. 19

a) Read the sentences about Ali's plans. <u>Underline</u> the simple present and (circle) the will-future.

1 If it <u>rains</u>, he'll travel by bus, but if <u>it's</u> sunny, he'll ride a city bike.

2 If he <u>travels</u> by bike, he'll have lunch in St James's Park.

3 If <u>it's</u> a Sunday, the museum won't be open.

4 If the museum <u>is</u> closed, he'll go to Camden Market with Pearl.

5 If he <u>sees</u> pelicans in St James's Park, he'll feed them.

6 If Ali and Pearl <u>go</u> to Camden Market, they'll buy lunch from the food stalls.

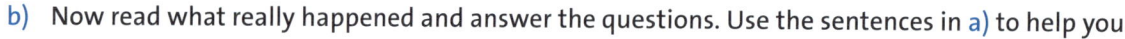

b) Now read what really happened and answer the questions. Use the sentences in a) to help you.

On Sunday, it rained.

1 Where did Ali go?   *He went to Camden Market (with Pearl).*

2 How did he travel?   *He travelled by bus.*

3 Where did he eat?   *He ate at the food stalls in Camden Market.*

9 LANGUAGE **London tips**   ▶ More help p. 31   ▶ SB, p. 19

Complete the conditional sentences with the correct verbs from the box.
Remember to use the simple present in the if-clauses and the will-future in the main clauses.

be (x3) • buy (x2) • cost • go • hurt • see • visit • walk • wear

1 If you *buy* _____ tickets for the London Dungeon online,

   they *'ll be* _____ cheaper.

2 If you *go* _____ to Buckingham Palace at 11 o'clock,

   you *'ll see* _____ the Changing of the Guards.

3 West End theatre tickets *will cost* _____ less if you *buy* _____ them on the day.

4 Your feet *won't hurt* _____ (not) at the end of the day if you *wear* _____ comfortable shoes.

5 If you *walk* _____ too slowly in the street, London people *won't be* _____ (not) happy!

6 The shops *won't be* _____ (not) too busy if you *visit* _____ on a weekday.

▶ Challenge 2, p. 32

10 Where will Lily go?

a) Read the directions. If Lily follows them from Charing C...

(handwritten note: ① my tour of London (PA / EA))

1   Take the first road on the right, then go straight over the roundabout at Tower and Neal Street. This place is on the right. *theatre*

2   Go straight on and take the second road on the left. This place is on the left. *bank*

3   Turn right at the shops. Take the first left, then go straight over the second roundabout. This place is on the right. *hospital*

4   Go straight on and turn right at the sports centre. Go straight on past the school, then turn left at the roundabout. This place is on the right. *library*

b) Write directions for Lily to get to Charles Road station.   ▶ Digital help

(Go straight on and turn right at the sports centre. Go straight on past the school. Go over the roundabout and it's on your right. / ...)

c) Partner A: You are Lily. Partner B choose a place on the map and give directions to Partner A. Does Partner A finish at the correct place? Then swap roles.   ▶ Early finisher 1, p. 30

I can **plan a tour.** ✓

☑ **11** WRITING **Rap Club** ► SB, p. 22

a) Write your own rap for Rap Club, about London or another city you know.
    Complete the rap lyrics with ideas from the colourful boxes or your own ideas.

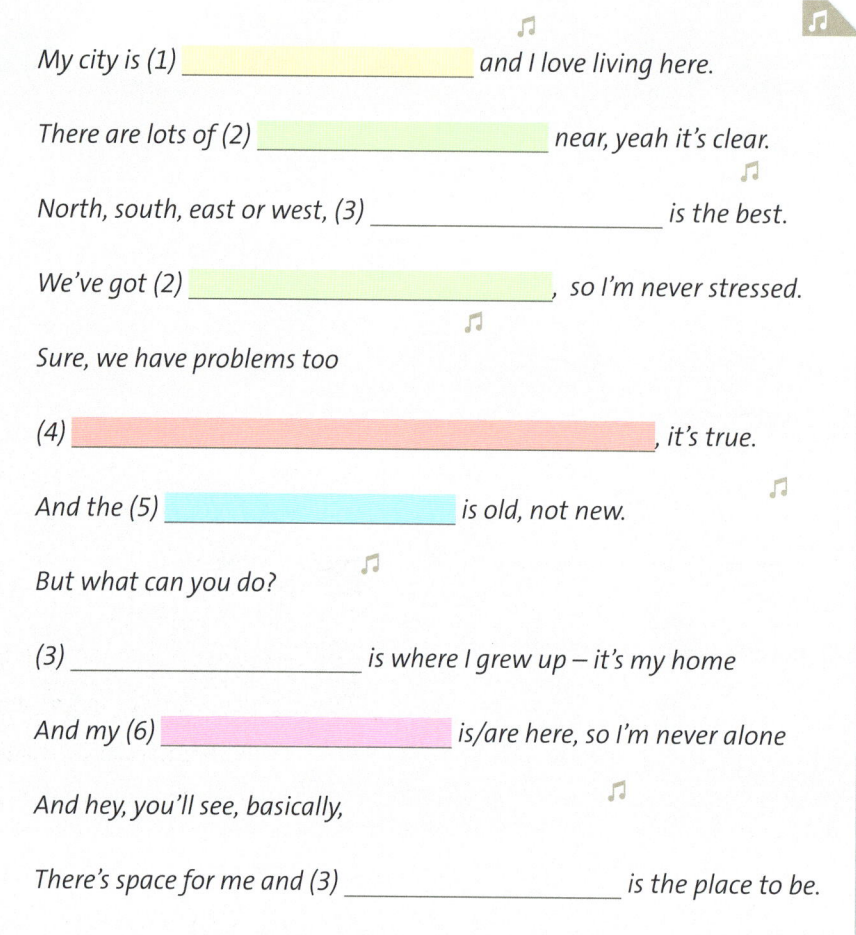

My city is (1) _____ and I love living here.

There are lots of (2) _____ near, yeah it's clear.

North, south, east or west, (3) _____ is the best.

We've got (2) _____, so I'm never stressed.

Sure, we have problems too

(4) _____, it's true.

And the (5) _____ is old, not new.

But what can you do?

(3) _____ is where I grew up – it's my home

And my (6) _____ is/are here, so I'm never alone

And hey, you'll see, basically,

There's space for me and (3) _____ is the place to be.

1 amazing, cool, fantastic, great
2 buses, cafes, museums, parks, people, shops, restaurants
3 no colour the name of your city
4 graffiti, homelessness, rubbish, traffic
5 castle, cinema, school, skatepark, swimming pool
6 family, friends

b) Read out or perform your rap to your partner.
    If you feel brave, you can also perform it to a group or to the class!

12 Reading Green Gym[1]

▶ SB, p. 23

a) **Read the website and the sentences 1–6. Are the sentences true (T) or false (F)?**

1 It's expensive to join Green Gym. `F`

2 Green Gym is a project to help the environment. `T`

3 Green Gym helps other people in the area. `T`

4 Green Gym projects take place in a building. `F`

5 Green Gym can help you in different ways. `T`

6 You need to be very fit to join Green Gym. `F`

---

www.greengymgroup.example.com

GREEN GYM: HELP THE ENVIRONMENT[2] AND YOUR BODY

If you want to keep fit, you can pay lots of money for fitness classes or you can join an expensive gym. Or … you can join a local Green Gym group and help the environment at the same time!

There are lots of Green Gym groups across London and the rest of the UK, so if you look at the map on our website, you'll find a group near you. We meet every week to do activities to help make our area greener. For example, we plant[3] trees, pick up rubbish and grow food in community gardens for local people. It's hard work, so if you help our team, you'll get just as much exercise as at the gym – but it's free and more fun! And the best bit is that you'll help the environment too.

Green Gym is good for you too, and not just fitness. It's a great way to make new friends. And you'll feel happier if you spend time outside every week.

We have lots of different projects, so you can help in the best way for you, and it doesn't matter if you're not very fit yet. Email us today to join!

---

b) **Complete the sentences and give your opinion.**

▶ More help, p. 32

I think Green Gym is *(great / a good project / …)*

because *(you can make the local area better. / …)*

I would like to / I don't want to join Green Gym because *(I want to help the environment. / I don't want to plant trees. / …)*

---

[1] **gym** *das Fitnessstudio* [2] **environment** *die Umwelt* [3] (to) **plant** *pflanzen*

13 SPEAKING **What's on the menu?**

► SB, p. 24

You and your partner visit a cafe in London, but there's a problem with the menus.
Partner B: Look at page 90.
Partner A: Ask your partner for the missing information and complete your menu.

> How much is ...?

> What costs £ ...?

> What's in a ...?

Greg's Breakfast Cafe

Big English breakfast (bacon[1], eggs, sausage, mushrooms[2], baked beans)	_£7.50_	**Turkish breakfast** (_bread_ , hummus, _olives_ , _eggs_ , tomatoes)	£6.50
Vegetarian English breakfast (_eggs_ , mushrooms, _tomatoes_ , baked beans)	£6.25	**Muesli with milk or yoghurt**	£2.25
		Fruit salad	_£2.75_
Eggs on toast	_£3.50_	**Tea or coffee**	£1.75
Pancakes	£3.25	**Fruit juice**	_£1.50_
Toast with butter and _jam_	£2.00	**Sparkling water**	£1.50

14 LISTENING **Pearl and Brianna's weekend**

► SB, p. 25

🔊 04

a) **Pearl's sister Brianna is talking to her grandma on the phone. Listen and circle the correct answer.**

1 Pearl and Brianna had a visit from their ...
   P friends.   **(M)** family.   L grandma.

2 In Trafalgar Square, they saw ...
   (E) paintings.   B musicians.   J street art.

3 Brianna ... the restaurant.
   W didn't know   Y didn't like   **(C)** loved

4 One evening, they went to ...
   (A) the theatre.   O the river.   U the cinema.

5 They couldn't go to the museum because ...
   V it was closed.   H it was too far.   **(N)** there wasn't time.

6 Brianna wants to take grandma ...
   F on a tour.   **(D)** on a boat trip.   E shopping.

b) **The six correct letters in a) form Brianna's favourite place in London:** _Camden_

---

[1] **bacon** _der Speck_   [2] **mushroom** _der Pilz_

I can **describe life in cities and in my area.** ✓

🖥 15 VIEWING **How to make a difference** ▶ SB, p. 29

Look at the tips from the video (1–3) and match them to the correct quotes (A–C).
Then watch the video and check.

1 Involve others.	C
2 It's good to talk.	A
3 Help others, help yourself.	B

A Even if you don't have money, speaking to people and asking them about their day will make people smile.

B Helping people has made Josh happy.

C One person who saw Josh's posts is Jade, a vet who wanted to help.

🖥 16 VIEWING **Josh's project** ▶ SB, p. 29

Watch the first 35 seconds of the video again and write the missing words.

Josh Coombes is a (1) *hairdresser* who wants to make a (2) *small* difference

to people's lives. He volunteers his time and skills, giving (3) *free* haircuts to the

homeless.

'I'm a hairdresser and I've been going out on the (4) *street* to cut hair for those who are

homeless.'

Josh started a project called *Do Something for* (5) *Nothing*. He wants to show people that

(6) *helping* others is good for the community and makes you (7) *feel*

good too.

17 **Before and after** ▶ SB, p. 29

Josh takes photos of the people he helps, so that more people can find out about the project.
Look at the photos and describe the man before and after his haircut.

Before the haircut, the man's hair was *(longer / untidier / …)*

and his beard[1] was *(longer / grey / …)*.

He looked *(sadder / older / …)*.

After the haircut, the man's hair is *(shorter / tidier / …)*

and his beard is *(shorter / gone / …)*.

He looks *(happier / smarter / younger / …)*.

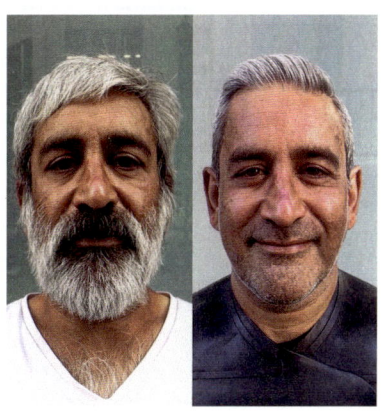

[1] **beard** *der Bart*

18 Words in Unit 1

a) Write the words in the puzzle.

1 You need this to travel on the river.

2 Lots of cars on the road.

3 Special moving stairs.

4 A type of transport with two wheels.

5 What people in London call the underground.

6 A direction to turn.

1	B	O	A	T					
2	T	R	A	F	F	I	C		
3		E	S	C	A	L	A	T	O	R
4		B	I	K	E				
5		T	U	B	E				
6		L	E	F	T				

b) Write a definition for the word in blue.

(Something you buy to travel on a bus or train.)

19 Word building

Use the puzzle pieces to build the correct words. You can use *-ful* and *-less* more than once.

1 When someone lives on the streets: *homeless*

2 When someone stays away from danger: *careful*

3 When someone is kind: *thoughtful*

4 When something never stops: *endless*

5 When something is red, blue, green: *colourful*

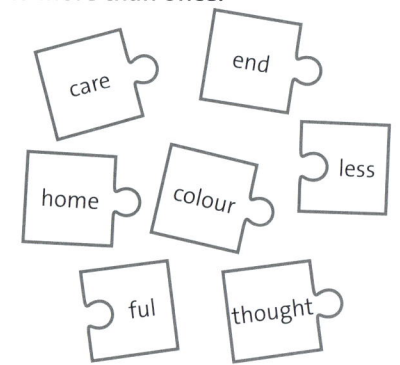

20 SPEAKING Speak English well: How do you say U?

▶ Digital help

a) How do you say the letter U in the words in the box?
Write them in the correct pronunciation categories.

 [ʌ] as in the word *up*.
[juː] as in the word *music*.

> bus • capsule • cucumber • public • sculpture • tube • Tuesday • tunnel • umbrella

1 [ʌ] *bus, cucumber, public, sculpture, tunnel, umbrella*

2 [juː] *capsule, cucumber, tube, Tuesday*

b) Now listen to the words. Were your answers in a) correct?
05

c) Listen and repeat the words from a).
06

My favourite exercise in Unit 1 was _____

because *(it was fun. / I like puzzles. / ...)* _____

I found these words and phrases in Unit 1 difficult:

_____

_____

I can remember:

Buckingham Palace

Places in London

bus

Transport

halloumi cheese

Food

stressful

Words with *-ful* and *-less*

My progress[1] in English:

💡 No one is perfect that is why pencils have rubbers.

Use the sentence builder to write about your confidence in English.

I feel most / very / quite confident about I feel least / don't feel very confident about	reading writing speaking listening	
I find		easy / the easiest difficult / the most difficult fun / the most fun

(I feel the most confident about reading, but I find writing the most

difficult. I feel quite confident about listening, but I find speaking difficult.

/ ...)

[1] **progress** *der Fortschritt*

Early finisher 1 **A crazy London tour**

a) Write a word for each of these categories.

1 a colour *(green)*

2 an animal *(elephant)*

3 a type of transport *(bike)*

4 a place in London *(Camden Market)*

5 a different place in London *(Big Ben)*

6 a type of food *(fish and chips)*

7 a famous person *(Adele)*

8 an adjective *(scary)*

9 a small number *(two)*

10 a big number *(999)*

b) Turn your workbook upside down and use your words from **a)** to complete the text.

> www.normaltours.example.com
>
> **(1)** *(Green)* **(2)** *(Elephant)* **Tours**
>
> Welcome to our London tour! You will travel by (3) *(bike)* and you will see lots of interesting places, like (4) *(Camden Market)*. We will stop for lunch at (5) *(Big Ben)* and you'll eat (6) *(fish and chips)*.
>
> The tour guide will be (7) *(Adele)* and he/she will tell you lots of (8) *(scary)* stories about London! The tour will last (9) *(two)* hours and will cost £(10) *(999)*.
>
> Call now to book!

c) Read your partner's tour. Then write your opinion of the tour.

I think the tour is *(funny / strange / stupid / ...)* .

I would like to go on this tour because *(I like the tour guide / I want to see Big Ben / ...)*

.

I don't want to go on this tour because *(it's too long / it's boring / it's too expensive / ...)*

.

▶ Check

Challenge 1 **London underground emoji quiz** ▶ WB, p. 20

Look at the London underground stations in the box, then write the correct station for each group of emojis. You don't need all the words from the box.

1 🐘🏰 _Elephant & Castle_

2 💰🏛️ _Bank_

3 👩🏽👩🏽👩🏽👩🏽👩🏽👩🏽 _Seven Sisters_

4 🍁💧 _Canada Water_

5 🟩🌳 _Green Park_

6 👸❌ _King's Cross_

7 🐶 _Barking_

8 ⬅️🍖 _West Ham_

> Angel • Bank • Barking • Camden Town • Canada Water • Charing Cross • Elephant & Castle • Green Park • King's Cross • Liverpool Street • Oxford Street • Piccadilly • Seven Sisters • Swiss Cottage • Victoria • West Ham

▶ Check ⤵

---

10 More help LANGUAGE **London tips** ▶ WB, p. 22 ▶ SB, p. 19

Complete the conditional sentences with the correct verbs from the box.

> buy (x2) • go • visit • walk • wear • will be • will cost • will see • won't be (x2) • won't hurt

1 If you _buy_ tickets for the London Dungeon online,

they _will be_ cheaper.

2 If you _go_ to Buckingham Palace at 11 o'clock,

you _will see_ the Changing of the Guards.

3 West End theatre tickets _will cost_ less if you _buy_ them on the day.

4 Your feet _won't hurt_ at the end of the day if you _wear_ comfortable shoes.

5 If you _walk_ too slowly in the street, London people _won't be_ happy!

6 The shops _won't be_ too busy if you _visit_ on a weekday.

Challenge 2 **Visiting my town**
▶ WB, p. 22

What will happen if Pearl and Ali visit your town? Complete the conditional sentences.

1 If it rains, we'll *(visit the History Museum.)*

2 If it's sunny, we'll *(have a picnic in the park.)*

3 If we get the bus, it will cost *(€1.60.)*

4 If they are hungry, we'll *(eat at my favourite Indian restaurant.)*

5 If I have time, I'll *(show them our big castle.)*

6 If *(they like shopping, we'll go to my favourite second hand shop.)*

7 If *(it's winter, we'll go to the Christmas market.)*

▶ Check

---

12 **More help** **Green Gym**
▶ WB, p. 25   ▶ SB, p. 23

b) **Use the ideas in the box to help you complete the sentences.**

I think Green Gym is	a good project / a bad project great / fantastic / OK / interesting / boring	
I would like to / don't want to join Green Gym because	you can I want to I don't want to	get fit / help the environment / make friends / plant trees / make the local area better
	you don't have to	pay any money / go to a gym / do projects that are too hard

I think Green Gym is *(great / a good project / ...)*

because *(you can make the local area better. / ...)*

I would like to / I don't want to join Green Gym because *(I want to help the environment. / I don't want to plant trees. / ...)*

1 London words

Write the words for the pictures, then find them in the wordsearch. The words can be in any direction.

F	U	O	G	I	C	T	E	L	U	R
C	L	N	B	P	T	I	C	A	T	O
L	I	F	T	E	O	L	A	N	E	U
K	T	C	I	S	U	B	L	D	A	N
E	Q	G	C	C	J	S	A	S	C	D
W	R	X	K	A	L	S	P	S	H	A
A	D	L	E	L	P	O	T	A	O	B
X	L	D	T	A	S	V	C	E	A	O
T	Y	P	D	T	S	K	L	K	M	U
B	W	Y	U	O	F	H	Z	L	W	T
U	N	D	E	R	G	R	O	U	N	D

1

boat

2

bus

3

clock

4

lift

5

king

6

ticket

7

roundabout

8

palace

9

escalator

10

underground

2 At the Lebanese cafe

 Erklär-film

Some customers are visiting Ali's grandparents' cafe.
Write the correct form of the verbs to complete the conditional sentences.

1 If you _like_ (like) spicy food, you _'ll love_ (love) the spicy sausages they do here!

2 I _'ll order_ (order) the chicken if I _have_ (have) enough money.

3 She _'ll have_ (have) the mango milkshake if it _'s_ (be) available[1].

4 If you _don't try_ (not try) the mint tea, you _'ll be_ (be) sorry because it's amazing!

5 If he _chooses_ (choose) the hummus, he _'ll order_ (order) some bread with it too.

6 You _won't like_ (not like) the kibbeh if you _don't eat_ (not eat) meat. ▶ Check

[1] **available** _verfügbar_

Unit 2
Manchester: Who we are

1 My hometown

▶ SB, p. 44

a) Omar's hometown Manchester is very important to him. How important is your hometown to you?

Not important at all   Very important

☐   ☐   ☐   ☐   ☐

b) Explain why. You can use the phrases in the box to help.

| I was/wasn't born here. I feel … here. | My friends/family are/aren't here. I want to live … | There's lots/not much to do. I think it's … |

My hometown is/isn't important to me because *(I feel happy here. / I want to live in a*

bigger city. / …)

2 Important things

▶ SB, p. 45

Complete the puzzle. The word in blue is something that is important to both Omar and Rosie.

1   A ball sport with eleven people on each team.

2   Where Omar and Rosie live.

3   The person you like to spend time with most. *(two words)*

4   How well you are.

5   When you're kind to people in sport. *(two words)*

6   Something you can use to text people or use the internet.

7   When you're nice to people.

1	F	O	O	T	B	A	L	L	
2	M	A	N	C	H	E	S	T	E	R
3	B	E	S	T	F	R	I	E	N	D
4	H	E	A	L	T	H			
5	F	A	I	R	P	L	A	Y	
6	P	H	O	N	E				
7	K	I	N	D	N	E	S	S	

Fashion

is important to both Omar and Rosie.

I can **explain what's important to me.** ✓

3 READING Rosie's friends

► SB, p. 46

Read the descriptions and circle the correct words.

1   Elena is wearing a **white /green** top and a patterned **skirt / dress**, plus black **trainers / glasses**.

2   Jacob is wearing a red **T-shirt / jumper**, **blue / black** jeans and red **headphones / glasses**.

3   Farida is wearing a **pink / red** T-shirt and a **scarf / jacket** in the same colour. She's also wearing **short / baggy** black trousers and long **white / black** boots.

4 LISTENING Manchester Fashion Week

► SB, p. 46

07

a)   **Listen to the description of a model. Draw the outfit. Listen again if you need to.**
   Then check page 47. How close is your picture?

b)   **What do you and don't you like about the outfit?**

I think this outfit is *(cool / interesting /*

old-fashioned / weird / ...).

I like the *(dress / hat / mix of styles /*

pockets / ...),

but I don't like the *(colours / trousers /*

trainers / ...).

► Early finisher 1, p. 46

5 Reading **Clothes swap**

► SB, p. 47

Read the article and answer the questions.

1 What does *Stitched Up* want to do? *(three answers)* *They want to help the planet, fight fast fashion and recycle clothes.*

2 How can you get free new clothes? *You can swap old clothes at a clothes swap.*

3 What rule is mentioned at this event? *You have to swap clothes that cost a similar price.*

4 What two things can you do if your clothes are broken? *You can take them to a repair event or learn to repair them.*

5 Which event isn't free? *The sewing course isn't free.*

6 What can you find on the website? *The sewing videos are on the website.*

www.sustainable-fashion.example.com/news

Don't shop, swap!

How many clothes do you have in your wardrobe that you never wear? The *Stitched Up* group in Manchester can help you make space, save money and look good – all while saving the planet! It's a charity that has regular events to fight the problems of fast fashion by recycling and reusing clothes.

For example, there's a clothes swap every month. This is the perfect way to get new outfits without spending any money. You can bring clothes that you don't wear any more, and you'll get a ticket for them. Then you can swap the ticket for different clothes that cost a similar price. That way, it's fair – you can't bring in a cheap hat and get designer jeans! But you can still find cool clothes you'll love. Mei Yoshida, 16, told us, 'I don't have enough money to buy new outfits all the time. But last week, I brought an old shirt that's too small for me to the swap, and I found a pretty skirt that's perfect for my friend's party at the weekend!'

What do you do if you get a hole[1] in your T-shirt? Don't throw it away – our planet doesn't need more rubbish! Bring it to one of the charity's repair events and their professionals can make it look as good as new. It's free because everyone is a volunteer. Or you can learn how to repair clothes yourself. S*titched Up* offers cheap sewing courses[2]. So you can make new clothes or update your old ones to keep them looking trendy. And if you can't go to a course every week, you can watch the videos on their website and learn at home.

Our city has lots of events like this, for example other clothes swaps at the Manchester Art Gallery. If you're not from Manchester, why not see if there's a similar charity in your local area. Let's stay in fashion AND save the planet together!

Source: https://stitchedup.coop (16.08.2023)

---

[1] **hole** *das Loch*   [2] (to) **sewing course** *der Nähkurs*

I can **talk about fashion.** ✓

6 READING **A letter to the *Hey!* advice column**

▶ SB, p. 49

Complete the letter with words from the box.

> buy • comfortable • dear • fashion • laugh • like • money • trendy

(1) *Dear* _____ advice column

All my friends have started wearing (2) *trendy* _____ new clothes, and they say I

should dress like them too. But we don't have a lot of (3) *money* _____ at home

and my parents won't (4) *buy* _____ me designer clothes because they say

(5) *fashion* _____ is a waste of money. I don't really (6) *like* _____

the latest fashion either, but I just want to fit in with my friends. I know some people at school

(7) *laugh* _____ at my old clothes, but they're (8)*comfortable* _____!

What can I do? – Sad student ☹

7 LANGUAGE **Answering the letter**

▶ SB, p. 51

Erklär-film

a) Read the answer from the *Hey!* advice column to the letter in exercise 6 and ⟨circle⟩ the correct words.

Dear Sad student

It's hard when you feel different, but you⟨**needn't**⟩/ **have to** change your clothes just because other people say you⟨**must**⟩/ **are allowed to** dress the way they want you to.

You **mustn't /**⟨**have to**⟩talk to your parents about this problem – you⟨**mustn't**⟩/ **are allowed to** keep it all inside. Maybe you can find a solution together. For example, you⟨**could**⟩/ **may** get a weekend job and earn some money that you **must /**⟨**are allowed to**⟩spend on anything you like.

But remember, with really good friends, you don't **mustn't /**⟨**have to**⟩be uncomfortable to make them happy. You⟨**could**⟩/ **needn't** talk to your friends and tell them how you feel. If they won't listen, then maybe instead of new clothes, you need new friends!

Best wishes – The *Hey!* advice column

b) What do you think about the advice?

(I think the advice is good because it's important to talk to people about your problems. / It's bad because making new friends is difficult.)

8 MEDIATION **What does it mean?** ▶ Digital help 👆   ▶ SB, p. 51

Your friend at school wants to understand the letter and answer from page 37. Explain in German.

Die Person ist traurig, weil *sie dazugehören will, sich aber keine coolen Klamotten*

leisten kann. Und eigentlich mag sie ihre Kleidung und will ihren Stil nicht

ändern.

Das Magazin sagt, *dass sie sich treu bleiben soll und sich nicht für andere verstellen*

soll. Außerdem soll sie mit ihren Freunden und ihren Eltern ehrlich darüber

sprechen. Und falls sie doch neue Kleidung kaufen will, dann könnte sie sich

einen Wochenendjob suchen.

9 LANGUAGE **Signs** ▶ More help, p. 47   ▶ SB, p. 51

Write the meaning of these signs using *must*, *mustn't*, *don't have to* and *not be allowed to*.

1	2	3

You mustn't / aren't allowed to ride your bike.	*You must stop.*	*You must wash your hands.*

4	5	6
END OF QUIET ZONE		
You don't have to be quiet.	*You mustn't / aren't allowed to bring your dog.*	*You mustn't / aren't allowed to turn right.*

☒ **10** LANGUAGE **Omar and Rosie's rules and chores** ▶Digital help 📞 ▶SB, p.51

Read the lists and complete the sentences with the correct modal verbs: *must, mustn't, (don't/doesn't) have to, (not) be allowed to, should, shouldn't.*

Omar:

– Tidy your bedroom every month.
– Don't stay up late or eat in your bedroom!!
– You can watch TV before bed.
– Please empty the dishwasher after school if you can.
– Vacuum the living room!

Rosie:

– Tidy your bedroom every week!!
– You can stay up late at weekends if you want.
– Don't watch TV every day or eat in your bedroom!!
– Please don't empty the dishwasher.
– Vacuum your room.

1 Rosie *must* tidy her bedroom every week,

but Omar *doesn't have to* do that – that's why it's always messy!

2 Omar *mustn't/isn't allowed to* stay up late, but Rosie *is allowed to* go to

bed late at weekends.

3 Rosie *mustn't/isn't allowed to* watch TV every day, but Omar *is allowed to* .

4 Omar *should* empty the dishwasher every day after school,

but Rosie *shouldn't* because she always drops the plates.

5 Omar *must* vacuum the living room,

but Rosie *doesn't have to* vacuum the living room.

6 Omar and Rosie *aren't allowed to* eat in their bedrooms because they're too messy.

7 Rosie and Omar *don't have to* cook dinner.

---

11 WRITING **My rules** ▶More help, p.48 ▶SB, p.51

What are you (not) allowed to do? What do/don't you have to do? Write at least three sentences.

(I'm allowed to go out late with my friends at the weekend, but I'm not allowed

to watch TV in my room. I have to take out the rubbish once a week, but I don't

have to babysit my little sister or cook. I must tidy my room every day.)

12 LANGUAGE Elena's competition

▶ SB, p. 53

a) **Rosie is talking to her friend Elena. Complete the conversation with words from the box.**

> each other (x2) • myself • ourselves • themselves • yourself

Rosie   Hey Elena, what's up? You look happy!

Elena   I'm so proud of (1) _myself_, Rosie – I've just won a skateboarding competition!

Rosie   That's brilliant! I've always believed in you and I hope you believe in (2) _yourself_ now too.

Elena   Well, it really wasn't easy at first, that's true. And last year, my friends and I all lost, and we were pretty hard on (3) _ourselves_. But we supported (4) _each other_ and now we're all much better skateboarders.

Rosie   They sound like great friends.

Elena   They are! They don't only think about (5) _themselves_. We all care about (6) _each other_.

b) **Complete the sentences about skateboarding with a reflexive pronoun or *each other*.**

1   Elena really enjoys _herself_ when she goes skateboarding.

2   Her skateboarding friends help _each other_ to do their best.

3   Elena's friend Kai hurt _himself_ last week when he fell over.

4   All the skateboarders were proud of _themselves_ even if they didn't win the last competition.

5   Being a good sportsperson means you shouldn't just think about _yourself_.

6   Elena says, 'I feel good about _myself_ when I know I've tried hard.'

7   Doing a sport that we love can help us have more confidence in _ourselves_.

🔊 **13** LISTENING **A confident Lioness**[1] ▶ SB, p. 53
08

a) Omar's friend Dev talks about Hannah Blundell. Read the sentences and listen.
Are the sentences true (T) or false (F)?

1 Dev doesn't like Hannah Blundell. **F**

2 The women's England football team is called the Lionesses. **T**

3 Hannah has always been good at football. **F**

4 She scored a goal for her first team. **F**

5 Chelsea didn't want Hannah to play for them at first. **T**

6 Hannah decided not to try to play for Chelsea after that. **F**

7 Hannah plays for Manchester United now. **T**

b) Listen again and correct the false sentences from a).

1 Dev likes Hannah Blundell.

3 Hannah hasn't always been good at football. / Hannah wasn't good at

football when she was young.

4 She never scored a goal for her first team.

6 Hannah tried again to play for Chelsea. / Hannah played for Chelsea when

she was 19.

c) Listen again and make notes. What problems and successes did Hannah have?

Problems	Successes
She didn't score a goal for her first team.	*She joined Chelsea at 19.*
She was too short to join the under-12 team of Chelsea Football Club.	*She joined Manchester United.*
	She won a prize for Player of the Season.

▶ Challenge 1, p. 48

---

[1] **lioness** *die Löwin*

👥 **14** SPEAKING **Ways to be more confident**   ▶ SB, p. 55

a) Omar has found two adverts for helping people with their confidence. Work with a partner.
Partner B: Look at page 90.
Partner A: Ask your partner these questions and write the answers.

1   What's the advert for? *It's for a 'confidence club' at school.*

2   How can it help people be more confident? *They can learn acting, dancing and talking in public.*

3   When can people do this? *Every Thursday at lunchtime.*

4   How can they try this club? *They should speak to Mrs Gibson to join.*

b) Read the advert and then answer your partner's questions.

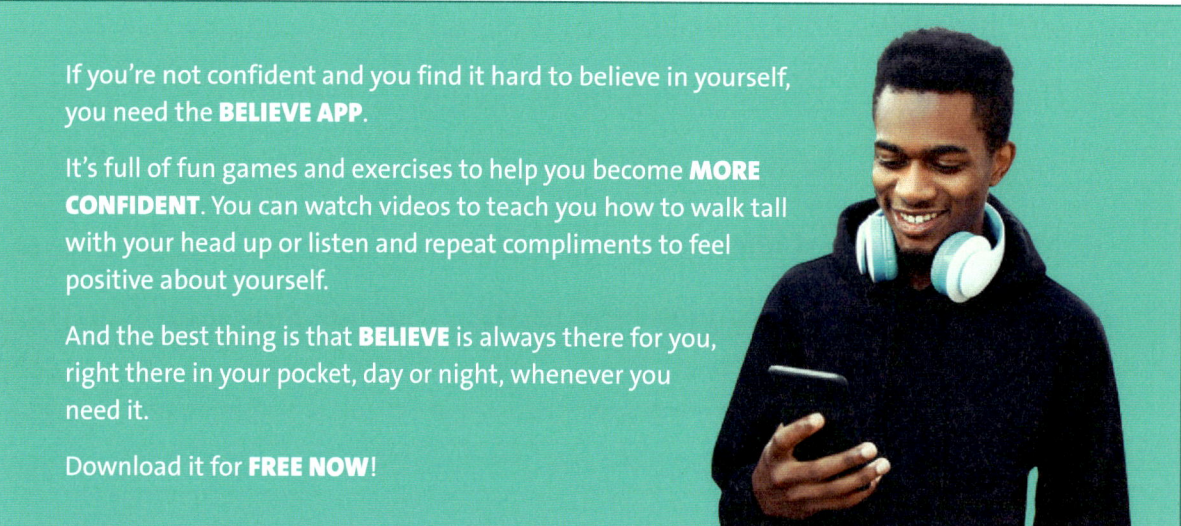

If you're not confident and you find it hard to believe in yourself, you need the **BELIEVE APP**.

It's full of fun games and exercises to help you become **MORE CONFIDENT**. You can watch videos to teach you how to walk tall with your head up or listen and repeat compliments to feel positive about yourself.

And the best thing is that **BELIEVE** is always there for you, right there in your pocket, day or night, whenever you need it.

Download it for **FREE NOW**!

c) Which activity do you think is best and why? Write the answer and compare with your partner.
(I like the app best because you can use it any time. / I don't like acting. / I like the 'confidence club' best because you can make friends. / I like dancing. / ...)

📝 **15** WRITING **Compliments**   ▶ SB, p. 55

Write one or two nice things about a friend in their workbook, and ask them to write something nice about you here. Come back to this page and read it when you need some confidence.

(You're good at maths. / You're a kind friend. / You try hard. / ...)

I can **talk about confidence.** ✓

16 READING **Who, what, where, how, why?**

▶ SB, pp. 56–58

Answer the questions about the story on **pages 56–57** in your book.

1 Which teams do Omar and Trent support? <u>Omar supports Manchester City and Trent supports Manchester United.</u>

2 Where does the story take place? <u>At a football match. / In Manchester.</u>

3 How did Omar and Trent talk during the match? <u>They texted each other.</u>

4 Why were some fans unhappy after the match? <u>Because their team lost.</u>

5 Who is Ollie? <u>He's Trent's cousin.</u>

6 What did Ollie do? <u>He called Omar and his family racist names and pushed Omar's dad.</u>

17 **Words in the story**

▶ SB, pp. 56–58

Find the football words in the story for each definition.

1 Someone who really likes a particular football team: <u>supporter / fan</u>

2 Where a football match is played: <u>stadium / pitch</u>

3 The footballer who stops goals: <u>goalkeeper</u>

4 Part of a goal: <u>net</u>

5 How many goals each team has got: <u>score</u>

6 When the match takes a bit longer: <u>additional time</u>

⊠ 18 WRITING **Your opinion**

▶ SB, pp. 56–58

What do you think about the end of the story? Do you agree with Omar's choice?

<u>(It was a difficult situation for Trent and Omar. But I think Trent made the wrong decision and chose his family although they were horrible to Omar. But then he made the right choice and said sorry to Omar. It's good that Omar wants to keep his friendship, but they also need to talk about what happened.)</u>

▶ Challenge 2, p. 48

19 Wrong word!

Which word is wrong? Why?

1 dress shirt skirt wear

Wear is wrong because *it's a verb. / not an item of clothing.*

2 trendy beautiful old-fashioned comfortable

Old-fashioned is wrong because *it's negative.*

3 friend problem enemy boyfriend

Problem is wrong because *it isn't a person.*

4 strict annoying kind shout

Shout is wrong because *it isn't an adjective. / it's something you do.*

5 burger stadium goalkeeper half-time

Burger is wrong because *it isn't a football word. / it's a type of food.*

20 SPEAKING Speak English well: F and V

🔊 09 a) **Listen to the words 'ferry' and 'very', and repeat.**

🔊 10 b) **Listen to the words and write if they have an F sound or a V sound.**

Remember:
English V sounds like **German W**

1 *F*	2 *V*	3 *V*	4 *F*	5 *V*
6 *F*	7 *F*	8 *V*	9 *F*	10 *V*

🔊 10 c) **Listen to the words again and repeat.**

👥 ☑ d) **Tic-Tac-Toe: Play with a partner.**
Take turns to say a word, then colour in that box. Can you get three boxes in a row?

▶ Digital help ⤵

ferry	sa**f**e	o**ff**
gi**f**t	fi**v**e	sa**v**e
o**f**	**v**ery	gi**v**e

In Unit 2, I was most interested in learning about (Manchester / football / ...)

because (I want to visit Manchester. / I'm very sporty. / ...)

I can write a sentence with

– must: I must do my homework.

– mustn't: (I mustn't stay up too late. / ...)

– have to: (You have to go to football practice. / ...)

– don't have to: (We don't have to wear a uniform at our school. / ...)

– needn't: (You needn't get up early. / ...)

– (not) allowed to: (I'm not allowed to watch scary films. / ...)

– might / may: (We might go to the cinema tonight. / ...)

– could: (You could wear that dress to the party. / ...)

– should / shouldn't: (He shouldn't tell you what to do. / ...)

My progress[1] in English

Write one or two words about how you find each skill or area.
Use words from the box or your own ideas.

💡 Don't forget you are doing great.

📖 Reading: (easy / fun / ...)

📝 Writing: (difficult / important / ...)

🔊 Listening: (interesting / best / ...)

🗣 Speaking: (embarrassing / useful / ...)

🔀 Mediation: (fun / useful / ...)

📺 Viewing: (easy / not useful / ...)

🔤 Grammar: (most difficult / boring / ...)

best • boring • difficult • easy • embarrassing • fun • important • interesting • useful • worst

---

[1] **progress** der Fortschritt

Early finisher 1 **Fashion designer**

a) Draw your own ideas for a fashionable outfit or a uniform for a football team.

b) WRITING Write a description of someone wearing your outfit. ▸ Digital help
Remember to use adjectives, colours and to describe the different materials and patterns.

_____

_____

_____

_____

_____

_____

Early finisher 1 **Fashion designer**

_____

4 Manchester Fashion Week

▶ WB, p. 35 ▶ SB, p. 46

Look at the model from the Manchester Fashion Week. Was your drawing correct?
Then answer the questions on page 35.

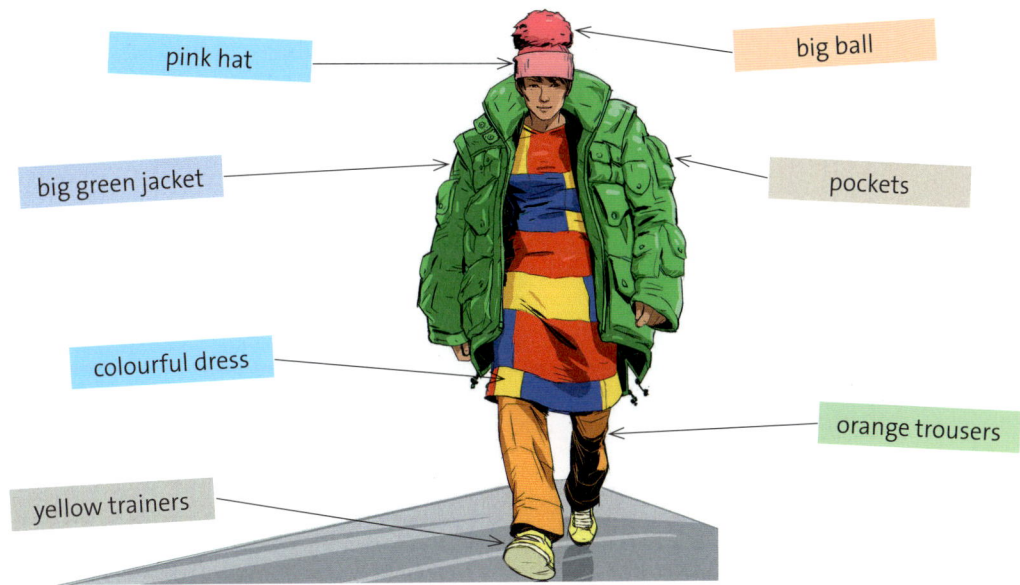

pink hat

big ball

big green jacket

pockets

colourful dress

orange trousers

yellow trainers

9 More help LANGUAGE Signs

▶ WB, p. 38 ▶ SB, p. 51

Complete the sentences. Use *must*, *mustn't*, *don't have to* and *not be allowed to*.

1

You mustn't / aren't allowed to ride your bike.

2

You *must* _____ _____ stop.

3

You *must* _____ _____ wash your hands.

4

You *don't have to* _____ _____ be quiet.

5

You *mustn't / aren't* _____ *allowed to* bring your dog.

6

You *mustn't / aren't* _____ *allowed to* _____ turn right.

---

11 More help My rules

▶ WB, p. 39 ▶ SB, p. 51

Use the modal verbs and ideas to help you write your about your rules.

I must / have to	tidy my ... / make my bed / do the ... / empty the dishwasher / cook / babysit (for ...) /
I mustn't / I'm not allowed to	stay up late / go out with ... / eat ... /
I don't have to / I'm allowed to	
I should / I shouldn't	watch TV (every day / in my room) / be nice to ...

Challenge 1 WRITING My role model

▶ WB, p. 41

Complete the sentences about your own role model.

My role model is _(Emma Raducanu)_ . He / She is _(a British tennis player)_ .

I admire him / her because _(she tries hard and never gives up)_ .

He / She shows confidence by _(talking about her feelings and being honest)_ .

I want to be _(brave)_ like him / her.

▶ Check

Challenge 2 WRITING Omar's problem

▶ WB, p. 43

Help Omar write an email to the *Hey!* advice column about what happened with Trent after the football match. Write 6–8 sentences.

www.hey-trafford-school.example.net/advice

Dear advice column

I have a problem with _(my friend. We went to a football match and my team won! But then some fans from the other team were very unhappy. My friend's cousin said some horrible, racist things to me and my family and he pushed my dad! But my friend didn't say anything. I don't know if I want to be his friend anymore.)_

What should I do? – Hurt student

▶ Check

1 Opposites

Write the opposite of these words from the unit.

1 friend ↔ *enemy*

2 trendy ↔ *old-fashioned*

3 colourful ↔ *plain*

4 throw away ↔ *reuse/recycle*

5 proud ↔ *ashamed*

6 confident ↔ *nervous*

7 agree ↔ *disagree*

8 baggy ↔ *tight*

Erklär-film

2 A good football fan

Omar is making a list of rules for being a good football fan at a match. Look at his notes and write the sentences using *must, mustn't, have to, don't have to, should, shouldn't, can* and *aren't allowed to.* Sometimes there's more than one possible answer.

> 1 ✓ ✗ sing songs to support your team
> 2 ✓ ✓ sit in the right part of the stadium
> 3 ✓ ✓ buy a ticket to the match
> 4 ✓   be respectful to other fans
> 5 ✓ ✗ buy food at half-time
> 6 ✗ ✗ use racist language
> 7 ✗ ✗ go on to the pitch
> 8 ✗   be mean if your team loses

1 You can/don't have to sing songs to support your team.

2 You must sit in the right part of the stadium.

3 You must/have to buy a ticket to the match.

4 You should be respectful to other fans.

5 You can/don't have to buy food at half-time.

6 You mustn't/aren't allowed to use racist language.

7 You mustn't/aren't allowed to go on to the pitch.

8 You shouldn't be mean if your team loses.

▶ Check

Unit 3
Scotland: Adventure

1 Places in Scotland

▶ SB, p. 75

a) Read the descriptions and write the correct places from the box on the map.

Ben Nevis • Edinburgh • Eilean Donan Castle • Inverness • Loch Ness • west coast

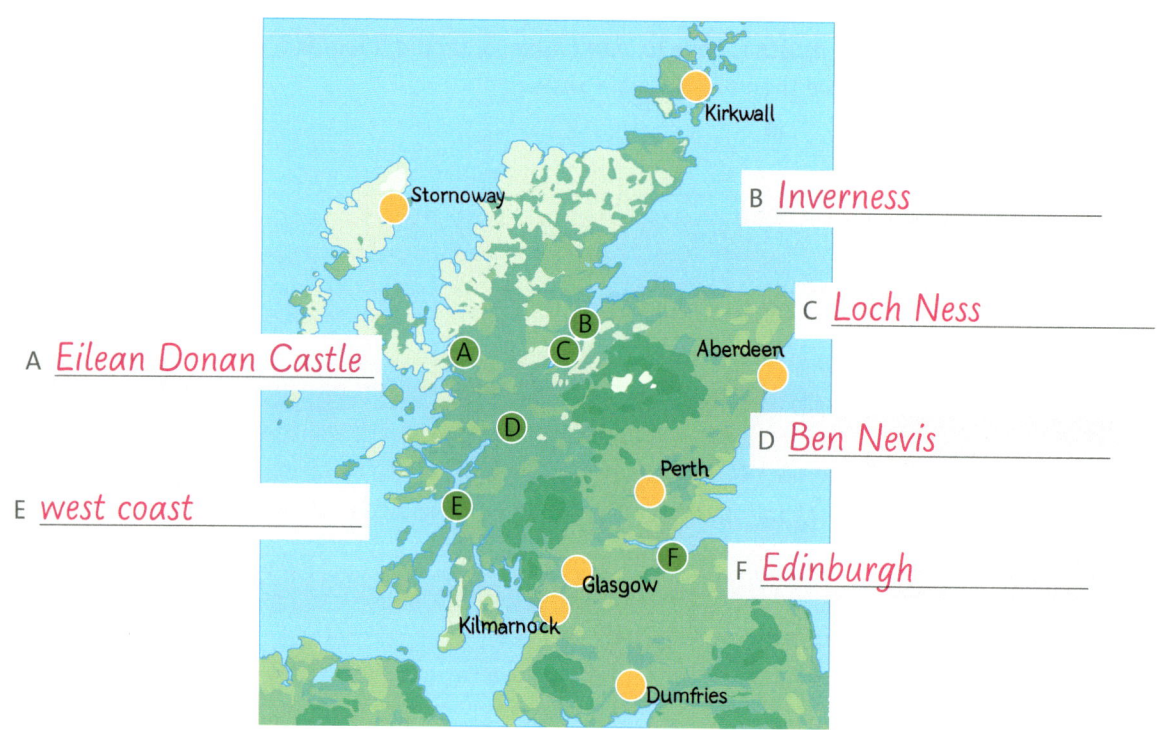

A Eilean Donan Castle

B Inverness

C Loch Ness

D Ben Nevis

E west coast

F Edinburgh

A This is a castle which might have a ghost in it!	B This is the city where Grace and Rhona live.
C This is a big lake. Some people think there's a monster in it!	D This is the tallest mountain in Scotland.
E This is a part of Scotland where you can go kayaking.	F This is the capital of Scotland. There's a castle and lots of shops for tourists here.

b) Look at the map and find the Scottish towns and cities.

1 This town is in the south of Scotland, near England: Dumfries

2 This city is on the east coast of Scotland: Aberdeen

3 This is the largest city in Scotland and is in the west: Glasgow

4 This is a town on an island in the north of Scotland: Kirkwall

I can **talk about Scotland.** ✓

🔊
11

2 LISTENING Looking for Nessie

▶ SB, p. 77

a) Listen to the radio report[1] and tick (✓) the correct box for each person.

	doesn't believe in Nessie	isn't sure	believes in Nessie
Rory			✓
Rory's dad John		✓	
Douglas			✓
Morag from Loch Ness Exploration			✓
The reporter	✓		

b) Listen to the report again and complete the notes.

▶ More help, p. 63

1   The legend of the Loch Ness Monster is very <u>old</u>. Hundreds of

people went to Loch Ness one weekend to <u>look for her</u> and more people

watched <u>online/the livestream</u>.

2   One boy called Rory said he thought that Nessie was <u>shy</u>. His dad

said that he didn't want to <u>know if Nessie was real</u>.

3   Some people saw a <u>monster</u> on the screen of their machine, but

actually it was <u>a fake monster from a film</u>.

c) What do you think about the search for Nessie? Do you think it's a fun idea to search for monsters? Why or why not?

<u>(I think the search is stupid because Nessie isn't real. / I think it's a fun idea to</u>

<u>search for monsters because we don't know what we will find. / ...)</u>

⬤
⬤
⬤

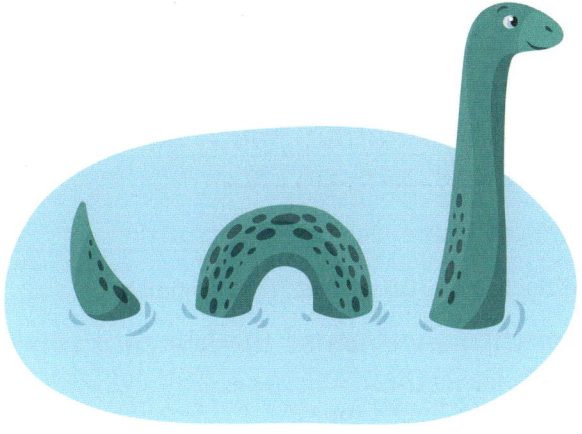

---

[1] **radio report** der Radiobericht

3 The legend of the Blue Men of the Minch

▶ SB, p. 79

a)   READING   Read the play and (circle) the four correct sentences.

1.   Lorna and Jamie are Finlay's granddaughter and grandson.

2.   Finlay says they shouldn't go to the Minch Sea.

3.   Finlay doesn't believe in the Blue Men of the Minch.

4.   The Blue Men of the Minch can be dangerous for people in boats.

5.   Jamie is rude to the Blue Man.

6.   The Blue Man wants them to tell him a poem.

7.   The Blue Man likes what Lorna says.

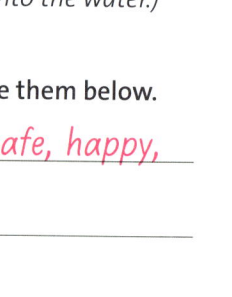

Scene 1

(Jamie and his sister Lorna are carefully *packing for a fishing trip[1].)*

Finlay	Where are you going fishing today, Jamie and Lorna?
Jamie	In the Minch Sea, near the island of Lewis, Grandad.
Finlay	Be careful, then. That's the home of the Blue Men of the Minch.
Lorna	*(curiously)* Are they real, Grandad?
Finlay	Aye, they are. They're strange creatures with blue bodies, and they'll sink your boat if you treat them badly. But they love to hear poems.

Scene 2

(Jamie and Lorna are at sea, but there's a storm and they are trying hard *to keep the boat safe. A Blue Man comes out of the water, singing* beautifully*.)*

Lorna	The Blue Men of the Minch! They're real!
Jamie	*(politely)* Please don't sink our boat, Blue Man. We are only fishing for food to eat.
Blue Man	*(singing)* We will keep you safe this time if you can make up a rhyme.
Jamie	*(quietly to Lorna)* That's right – Grandad Finlay said the Blue Men love poems. We need to think of a poem fast!
Lorna	*(thinks for a moment then shouts* confidently*)* The sky is blue, the sun is warm. Oh, Blue Man, please don't call a storm. We always take care of the sea, so please let us get home safely.
Blue Man	*(singing* happily*)* Because you show respect for our waters. You can go free, young son and daughter. *(The Blue Man swims* silently *down into the water.)*
Jamie	Well done, Lorna!

Erklär-
film

b)   LANGUAGE   Highlight all the adverbs in the play. Then turn them into adjectives and write them below.

careful, curious, bad, hard, beautiful, polite, quiet, fast, confident, safe, happy,

silent

c)   What do you think about the legend? Do you like it? Why (not)?

(I think the legend of the Blue Men of the Minch is interesting. / boring. / (not)

true. / … I like it because I love legends. / …)

---

[1]   **fishing trip** *der Angelausflug*

4 LANGUAGE **Adverbs**

▶ SB, p. 79

Turn the adjectives from the box into adverbs. Then write the adverbs in the puzzle to find a Scottish city.

angry • fast • good •
hungry • polite • sad • safe

The Scottish city is *Glasgow* .

1	A	N	G	R	I	L	Y		
2	S	A	D	L	Y				
3			F	A	S	T			
4			S	A	F	E	L	Y	
5	H	U	N	G	R	I	L	Y	
6			P	O	L	I	T	E	L	Y
7			W	E	L	L			

5 LANGUAGE **Scottish ghosts**

▶ More help, p. 63   ▶ SB, p. 79

Look at the pictures and choose an adverb to complete each sentence.

The Grey Lady is singing
beautifully/well .

The soldier is walking
fast/quickly .

The little boy is crying
sadly .

The girl in the white dress is
laughing *happily* .

The headless man is carrying his
head *carefully* .

Greyfriars Bobby is barking
angrily .

▶ Early finisher 1, p. 62

I can **understand stories and legends.** ✓

6 Sports

▶ Digital help ▶ SB, p. 80

Complete the Venn diagram with the sports in the box. One sport doesn't fit in the diagram.

basketball • cliff jumping •
cold water swimming •
football • hiking •
ice hockey • kayaking •
skiing • snowboarding •
surfing • underwater hockey

football

basketball

Team sports

hiking

underwater hockey

ice hockey

kayaking

snowboarding

Water sports

cold water swimming

Winter sports

surfing

skiing

cliff jumping

7 SPEAKING A brochure

▶ SB, p. 80

a) This is a timetable from a brochure for an adventure sports centre. Some information is missing.
Partner B: Look at page 91.
Partner A: Ask your partner for the missing information and answer their questions.

What can you do on (day) at (time) ...?

How much does ... cost?

	9 o'clock		**12 o'clock**		**3 o'clock**	
Monday	paddle boarding	£10	skiing	£30	swimming	£5
Tuesday	snowboarding	£30	kayaking	£15	mountain biking	£25
Wednesday	cliff jumping	£20	mountain biking	£25	snowboarding	£30
Thursday	swimming	£5	paddle boarding	£10	cliff jumping	£20
Friday	kayaking	£15	swimming	£5	skiing	£30

b) Decide with your partner which three activities you would both like to do. When are they and how much will it cost in total?

8 A young adventurer

▶ SB, p. 83

Erklär-
film

a) LANGUAGE **Read the article and write the verbs in the present perfect.**

A young mountain adventurer

Quinn Young, a 10-year-old girl from Inverness, (1) *has become* (become) one of the youngest people in the world to climb all the Munros in Scotland.

A Munro is a Scottish mountain that is over 3,000 feet or 914 metres high. Many hikers challenge themselves to climb them all – but little Quinn (2) *has managed* (manage) it at a much younger age than most!

She (3) *has climbed* (climb) mountains almost all her life, starting at age four with her dad, Ian, and she reached the top of Ben Nevis just before she turned five.

She carries all her own water, food and spare clothes, and she (4) *has never complained* (never complain), even in bad weather, her dad explained.

Over 7,000 people (5) *have finished* (finish) the challenge officially, climbing all 282 Munros in Scotland, but most of them were adults[1]. Now Quinn can join this list of adventurers. She and

Ben Nevis

her dad (6) *haven't tried* (not try) to climb Mount Everest yet, but we're sure Quinn can do it!

b) READING **Read the article again and correct the sentences.**

1 Quinn Young is the youngest person ever to climb all the highest mountains in Scotland.

   Quinn Young is one of the youngest people ever to climb all the highest mountains in Scotland.

2 She climbed Ben Nevis when she was five.

   She climbed Ben Nevis when she was four.

3 Her dad carries her equipment.

   She carries her own equipment.

4 282 people have climbed all the Munros in Scotland.

   Over 7,000 people have climbed all the Munros in Scotland.

5 Quinn and her dad have climbed Mount Everest.

   Quinn and her dad haven't climbed Mount Everest.

---

[1] **adult** *der/die Erwachsene*

Erklär-film

12

9 LANGUAGE Present perfect with *for* and *since*

▶ SB, p. 83

a) LISTENING Isla works at the Adventure Centre that Grace and Rhona's class are visiting. Read the sentences 1–5 and look at the timeline. Then listen to Isla and write a–e in the boxes next to the sentences.

She has worked at the Adventure Centre.   `b`

She has been interested in adventure sports.   `e`

She has done snowboarding.   `d`

She has done cliff jumping every summer.   `c`

She has taken paddleboarding lessons.   `a`

Isla was 7   Isla was 15   8 years ago   6 years ago   December last year   now

a

b

c

d

e

b) Complete the phrases from the listening with *for* or *since*.

1 *since* she was 7

2 *since* she was 15

3 *for* 8 years

4 *for* 6 years

5 *since* December last year

10 LANGUAGE Your experiences

▶ SB, p. 83

Write five sentences about how long you have done different things using *for* and *since*. You can use the phrases in the box to help you.

be	friends with (name) / vegan / ...
do	a hobby / a course / ...
have	a pet / a phone / a bike / ...
play	an instrument / a sport / ...

1 I have been at my school *(for three years. / ...)*

2 I have lived in my house *(since I was a baby. / ...)*

3 I have *(been a vegetarian for a year. / ...)*

4 *(I have played the guitar since I was 10. / ...)*

5 *(I have had a cat for two months. / ...)*

I can **talk about adventures and interests.**

11 WRITING **Problems in nature**

▶ More help, p. 64   ▶ SB, p. 84

Some people have not followed the tips for protecting nature.
Look at the picture and say what somebody has done.
Write the sentences.

Five sentences – good!
Six sentences – great!

1 Somebody has <u>*left the gate open.*</u>

2 <u>*Somebody has made a fire.*</u>

3 <u>*Somebody has left rubbish.*</u>

4 <u>*Somebody has fed the animals.*</u>

5 <u>*Somebody has picked flowers.*</u>

6 <u>*Somebody has left the path.*</u>

12 MEDIATION How to help

▶ SB, p. 84

Read the advert and sum it up in German.

Help protect birds in your area

The number of different types of birds has gone down across Scotland, and our birds need your help! Luckily, there are things you can do:

- Leave out nuts[1], seeds[2], fruit, fat and grain[3] for them to eat, plus fresh water for drinking and cleaning. But don't do this if you have a cat!
- Don't feed wild birds bread or rice as it's not healthy for them.
- Download our app and send photos of birds in your area to help us with our research.

(Die Artenvielfalt der Vögel in Schottland ist zurückgegangen. Man kann den Tieren helfen, indem man Futter auslegt, aber nur wenn man keine Katze hat. Nüsse und Samen sind z. B. geeignete Nahrung für Vögel, Brot oder Reis sind schlecht für Vögel. Und wenn man sich die App holt, dann kann man Bilder einsenden und damit der Forschung helfen.)

13 Nature in your area

▶ Digital help   ▶ SB, p. 85

a) Write the correct nature word for each picture, then tick (✓) the ones that are in your area.

| 1 *hill* ☐ | 2 *mountains* ☐ | 3 *lake* ☐ | 4 *river* ☐ |

| 5 *deer* ☐ | 6 *cows* ☐ | 7 *seagulls* ☐ | 8 *forest* ☐ |

b) Use an online dictionary: Write four more things you can find in your area. A type of ...

bird: *(pigeon /...)*   flower: *(daisy /...)*   animal: *(fox / ...)*   tree: *(oak /...)*

c) SPEAKING Tell your partner about your favourite place in nature in your area, what you can see there and why you like it.

---

[1] **nut** *die Nuss*   [2] **seed** *der Samen*   [3] **grain** *das Getreide*

I can **talk about nature.** ✓

14 VIEWING **What happens in the video**

▶ SB, p. 89

Read the text and circle the correct information. Then watch the video and check.

Mon lives in Scotland / Norway and has made a vlog about a boat trip / road trip. It's her first / second time in Scotland and it's strange for Mon and her friend George to drive on the right / left side of the road. In her vlog, Mon explores a lot of different castles / islands and then visits the city of Glasgow / Inverness. Mon and George swim / don't swim on the Isle of Skye because the water is cold / warm. Mon climbs down a valley / mountain to a small river, then on the last day, they listen to traditional music / poems.

15 **Words in the video**

▶ SB, p. 89

Write the correct words from the box.

| bagpipes • burn • cave • isle |

1   a small island: *isle*

2   a large hole in a mountain: *cave*

3   a small river in Scotland: *burn*

4   a Scottish musical instrument: *bagpipes*

16 WRITING **A scene from the video**

▶ SB, p. 89

Choose one of these scenes from the video and write five sentences about it.

Inverness

Dunnottar Castle

(2 This is Dunnottar Castle. It's the second castle Mon and George visit. It looks as if it was once a very big castle in the past. Some people are walking around the castle on the grass. There are dark clouds in the sky. / ...)

▶ Early finisher 2, p. 62

17 Words in Unit 3

Complete the crossword puzzle.

1   Like a plane, used for rescues in the mountains.

2   An old story that might not be true.

3   Land next to the sea.

4   Hill or mountain next to the sea.

5   Jumping out of a plane.

6   Someone who plays the bagpipes.

7   A creature who is half woman, half fish.

8   Enjoying exciting sports.

Crossword answers:
1. HELICOPTER
2. LEGEND
3. COAST
4. CLIFF
5. SKYDIVING
6. PIPER
7. MERMAID
8. ADVENTUROUS

18 Word families

▶ Digital help

Complete the word families in the table. Use an online dictionary if you need to.

verb	noun	adjective	adverb
	adventure	adventurous	adventurously
excite	excitement	exciting	excitingly
interest	interest	interesting	interestingly
protect	protection	protective	protectively

19 LISTENING Speak English well: Word stress

13

Listen to the words and underline the stressed[1] syllable[2].

1 Edinburgh

2 adventure

3 relax

4 unfortunately

5 submarine

6 valley

7 eventually

8 primary

▶ Challenge 1, p. 64

[1] **stressed** *betont*   [2] **syllable** *die Silbe*

Something new I learned about Scotland in Unit 3 is that: *(Some people think there's a monster in Loch Ness. / They use different words. / …)*

How confidently I can do these things

Write an adverb or a phrase for each of the *I can* statements. You can use ideas from the table or your own ideas.

confidently	not confidently
quite well very well	not very well yet
without help	with help

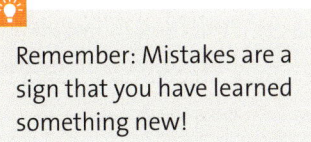

Remember: Mistakes are a sign that you have learned something new!

1   I can talk about Scotland *(confidently. /…)*

2   I can understand stories and legends *(very well. / …)*

3   I can talk about adventures and interests *(with help. / …)*

4   I can talk about nature *(not confidently. / …)*

5   I can discuss good and bad choices in a story *(quite well. / …)*

6   I can structure ideas for a story *(without help. / …)*

7   I can write a short adventure story *(very confidently. / …)*

My next steps

Choose two *I can* statements that you find more difficult and write how you are going to improve. You can use ideas from the box or your own ideas.

ask	my teacher / other students / …	for help / feedback / …
practise	speaking / … English	with other students / my parents / …
read	more in English	
listen	to English	in movies / games / …
use	a dictionary / an app	

I am going to *(ask my teacher for help with structuring ideas for a story. / I am going to look for discussion phrases in my book. / …)*

Early finisher 1 READING **A ghost hunter**

Read the ghost hunter's blog and answer the questions.

> Hi, I'm Sarah and my hobby is ghost hunting! About once a month, I go to a haunted house[1] with my friends – for example, Eilean Donan Castle or one of the underground tunnels in Edinburgh – and we stay awake all night, looking for ghosts!
>
> I've been a ghost hunter for five years now, but I've never seen a ghost walking around, I'm sure I've heard them. Once, we were in a very old house we heard footsteps[2] in the hall – but there was nobody else in the house! Another time, I saw a glass moving on a table, but nobody was touching it. I've also taken photos in dark, empty rooms and then found strange lights in the photos, which my friends said were ghosts.
>
> It's not for everyone, but I don't think people need to be scared when they go ghost hunting because I believe most ghosts are friendly and just want to say hello.

1 What do ghost hunters do?

   They stay awake all night in a haunted house and look for ghosts.

2 How long has Sarah done ghost hunting?

   She's done ghost hunting for five years.

3 Does Sarah believe in ghosts? Why (not)?

   Yes, because she says she has heard them and seen photos of them.

4 Is Sarah scared during ghost hunts? Why (not)?

   No, because she believes most ghosts are friendly.

5 Would you like to go ghost hunting? Why (not)?

   (Yes, because it sounds exciting. / ... / No, because ...)   ▶ Check 🔽

Early finisher 2 WRITING **My dream tour of Scotland**   ▶ Digital help 🔽

Plan your dream tour of Scotland. What will you see and do? Think about:

– places to visit and stay in	– sports, activities and day trips
– food and drink	– transport

(In my dream tour of Scotland, I'll travel everywhere by helicopter. I'll visit Edinburgh and go ghost hunting in the caste. I'll search for Nessie in Loch Ness. And I will go hiking on the Isle of Skye. I will climb Ben Nevis and go skiing in the mountains. I will try haggis and have some shortbread with tea.)

---

[1] **haunted house** *das Geister-, Gespensterhaus*   [2] **footstep** *der Schritt*

🔊
11

2 [More help] LISTENING **Looking for Nessie** ▶ WB, p. 51 ▶ SB, p. 77

b) Listen to the report again and circle the correct words.

1 The legend of the Loch Ness Monster is very recent / old. Hundreds of people went to Loch Ness one weekend to look for her / make a film about her and more people watched at the cinema / online.

2 One boy called Rory said he thought that Nessie was unfriendly / shy. His dad said that he didn't want to know if Nessie is real / see Nessie.

3 Some people saw a monster / fish on the screen of their machine, but actually it was the Loch Ness monster / a fake monster from a film.

5 [More help] LANGUAGE **Scottish ghosts** ▶ WB, p. 53 ▶ SB, p. 79

Look at the pictures. Use the adjectives in the box and turn them into adverbs to complete the sentences.

angry • careful • fast • good • happy • sad

The Grey Lady is singing

well.

The soldier is walking

fast.

The little boy is crying

sadly.

The girl in the white dress is

laughing _happily_.

The headless man is carrying his

head _carefully_.

Greyfriars Bobby is barking

angrily.

11 More help WRITING Problems in nature ▶ WB, p. 57 ▶ SB p. 84

Use the ideas to help you write your sentences. Don't forget to put the verbs in the present perfect.

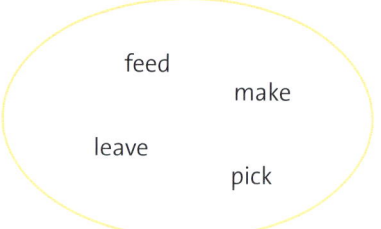

feed
make
leave
pick

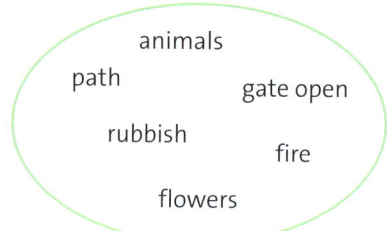

animals
path
gate open
rubbish
fire
flowers

Challenge 1 LISTENING Listen carefully! ▶ Digital help 🔽 ▶ WB, p. 60

🔊 14

a) Some English words change their stress[1] depending on if they are verbs or nouns.
Listen to the five sentences and <u>underline</u> the stressed syllable in the words in blue.

1   I'm going to download the game, but the
    download will take a lot of time.

2   If you progress quickly, it means you've made
    lots of progress.

3   I don't have a record of my work because I
    didn't record it.

	verb	noun
download	herunterladen	der/das Download
progress	vorankommen	der Fortschritt
record	dokumentieren	die Aufzeichnung
increase	zunehmen	der Anstieg
update	aktualisieren	das Update

4   There has been an increase in the number of people who have climbed Ben Nevis, and it will continue
    to increase.

5   You need to update your computer, then give me an update.

b) Look at the blue words in a) and (circle) the correct words.

When it's a noun, you stress[2] the (first) / second syllable.

When it's a verb, you stress the first / (second) syllable.

▶ Check 🔽

---

[1] **stress** *die Betonung*   [2] (to) **stress** *betonen*

1 Category[1] game

Find words for each of the categories and letters in the table.
Compare your answers with a partner. Who found the most words?

	nature words	sports	legend words	☒ adverbs
H	(heather, hill, ...)	(hiking, horse riding, ...)	(hero, ...)	(happily, hard, ...)
M	(mountain, ...)	(match, mountain climbing, ...)	(mermaid, monster, ...)	(monthly, mysteriously, ...)
S	(sand, sea, sky, ...)	(skiing, snowboarding, ...)	(scary, ship, ...)	(surprisingly, suddenly, ...)
W	(wilderness, wind, ...)	(walking, windsurfing, ...)	(witch, ...)	(well, wildly, ...)

2 A Scottish tour guide

Erklär-film

Read the text and circle the correct words.

Craig isn't from Scotland, but he has (1) **live** / **lived** in Edinburgh (2) **for** / **since** ten years, so he feels that it's his home. He's always (3) **been** / **was** interested in history, but (4) **for** / **since** the last six months, he has (5) **working** / **worked** as a ghost tour guide. He takes tourists around the city and tells them stories about some of the scariest buildings.

'I haven't (6) **saw** / **seen** a ghost myself, but I believe in ghosts,' he says. 'My favourite place to visit is Greyfriar's Kirkyard, which has (7) **had** / **have** a ghost of a dog called Bobby (8) **for** / **since** 1872. Lots of people have (9) **told** / **tell** me that they have (10) **hear** / **heard** the sound of a dog near the church.'

▶ Check

---

1 **category** *die Kategorie*

Unit 4
Wales: Digital life

1 What's wrong?

► SB, p. 107

Read the sentences about Wales. Cross out (~~cross out~~) the wrong word in each sentence and write the correct word.

1 Wales is in the ~~east~~ of Great Britain. *west*

2 The Welsh flag is green and white, with a ~~green~~ dragon. *red*

3 The national sport of Wales is ~~football~~. *rugby*

4 The capital of Wales is ~~Llandudno~~. *Cardiff*

5 Wales was an important area for ~~gold~~ mining. *coal*

2 Welsh cakes

► SB, p. 107

a) On St David's Day, the special day for Wales, many people make Welsh cakes. Complete the recipe.

add • bowl • cut • egg • fry • mix • stir

Ingredients

225 g	flour	85 g	sugar
1/2 spoon	baking powder	(A) 1	*egg*
110 g	butter	55 g	raisins[1]

First (B) *mix* the flour, baking powder and butter together in a (C) *bowl* with your fingers.

Then add the sugar and the egg and (D) *stir* the mixture. (E) *Add* the raisins and make a

dough[2] with your hands. Then roll[3] the dough and (F) *cut* out circles. Finally (G) *fry* the

circles in a pan for 3 minutes on each side until they are brown. You don't need any oil.

b) If you can, make Welsh cakes and write what you think of them.

I thought the Welsh cakes that I made were *(delicious. / easy to make. / ...)* ► Early finisher 1, p. 78

[1] **raisin** *die Rosine*   [2] **dough** *der Teig*   [3] **(to) roll** *ausrollen*

I can **understand information about Wales.** ✓

3 MEDIATION **Gwen's video**

► SB, p. 108

One of the students in the German exchange class has asked you to help them understand Gwen's video about Cardiff. Look at the screenshots and subtitles[1] and sum up in German.

	This is Cardiff, one of the smallest capital cities in Europe. It's a long way from Llandudno, but I sometimes visit it with my family.	*(Cardiff ist eine der kleinsten Hauptstädte Europas. Gwen besucht die Stadt manchmal mit ihrer Familie.)*
	Cardiff Castle is on a big hill in the middle of the city. You can go inside, and there's lots to see. I love climbing up the tower!	*(Das Cardiff Castle ist auf einem großen Hügel im Stadtzentrum. Im Schloss gibt es viel zu entdecken und auch einen Turm zu besteigen.)*
	There's always lots going on in the city centre. You'll find street musicians plus food and drink from all over the world!	*(Im Stadtzentrum gibt es viel zu erleben: Straßenmusik sowie Essen und Trinken aus aller Welt.)*
	I love the beach at Cardiff Bay, with beautiful, clean sand – even if the water is usually very cold!	*(Der Sandstrand ist schön und sauber, aber das Wasser ist meist sehr kalt.)*
	If you like shopping, Cardiff is perfect because there are lots of shopping centres, shops and a big indoor market.	*(Cardiff hat viele Einkaufszentren, Geschäfte und eine große Markthalle.)*

4 LANGUAGE **Is it yours?**

► SB, p. 108

Replace the blue phrases in the text with a possessive pronoun.

Owen found some sweets in the classroom. He asked Dylan, 'Are they (1) *yours* (your sweets)?'

But Dylan said no. Samara said they were (2) *hers* (her sweets), but Promit also said they were

(3) *his* (his sweets). In the end, Mr Price said sweets weren't allowed, so everyone said they

weren't (4) *theirs* (their sweets)! But really, they were (5) *mine* (my sweets) ...

---

[1] **subtitles** *die Untertitel*

5   READING   A bilingual[1] school

▶ SB, p. 109

a)   LANGUAGE **Read the blog post about life at a school in Wales and fill each gap with a possessive pronoun.**

My school / Fy ysgol

Hi, I'm Gareth and, like most young people in Wales, I learn Welsh at school – but in a different way! Lots of people have blogs about their school life, so here's (1) _mine_ .

Most schools have their lessons in English, but (2) _ours_ are different because our school is bilingual, so we have some lessons in English, but others in Welsh. For example, I learn maths in English but chemistry and biology in Welsh.

Apart from[2] the language, my lessons are probably just the same as (3) _yours_ – some are interesting, some aren't! My favourite subject is probably geography, but my sister says (4) _hers_ is music.

My grandparents are really happy about my school experience because (5) _theirs_ was so different. When they were young, lots of people didn't think it was useful to learn Welsh, so the language nearly died out. My parents can't really speak it. Sometimes that's a problem because they can't help me with my homework. However, it also means I have a secret language with my friends!

I'm so happy I can speak Welsh really well. More and more people speak it now, and I think it's a beautiful language. And it's boring if everyone just speaks English all the time!

So that's what my school is like. Leave a comment and tell me about (6) _yours_ !

b)   **Read the blog post again and tick (✓) the four correct statements.**

1 All of Gareth's lessons are in Welsh.	☐
2 Gareth learns science in Welsh.	☑
3 Gareth's sister doesn't like music.	☐
4 Gareth's grandparents didn't learn Welsh at school.	☑
5 Gareth's parents help him with his homework.	☐
6 Gareth's parents can't understand when he speaks to his friends in Welsh.	☑
7 Welsh has become popular.	☑
8 Gareth thinks everyone should speak English.	☐

c)   **Tell Gareth what you think about his school and which languages you learn at yours.**   ▶ Digital help

(I think a bilingual school is a great idea because you can learn a language really well. I learn English and French at school.)

---

[1] **bilingual** _zweisprachig_   [2] **apart from** _abgesehen von_

I can **talk about Wales.** ✓

6 LISTENING A digital detox[1]

▶ SB, p. 110

15

a) Listen to Mia's podcast and (circle) the correct answers.

1 Mia's project takes/took place ...
   A last week.   B this week.
   C next week.

2 A digital detox means ...
   A cleaning your devices[2].   **B** not using any devices.
   C only using green technology.

3 Mia's mum ...
   A uses her phone a lot too.   B doesn't have a phone.   C gets out a lot.

4 At weekends, Mia uses her devices for ...
   A more than 6 ½ hours.   B 6 ½ hours.   C half an hour.

5 Mia's family ...
   A doesn't support her.   **B** is going to join in the digital detox.   C doesn't have internet.

6 Maybe Mia will ...
   A listen to CDs.   B take her little sister to the park.   **C** read more.

b) Answer the questions in 1–2 sentences.

1 Do you think a digital detox is a good idea? Why or why not?

   (Yes, because I use my phone too much. / No, because devices are too useful. / ...)

2 How much screen time do you normally have each day? What do you think about this?

   (I have ... hours of screen time a day and I think this is fine. / too much because it's not healthy. / ...)

3 What do you think is the hardest thing about a digital detox?

   (I think the hardest thing is not texting friends or using social media, so you don't know what's happening. / ...)

c) Try a digital detox for a day! Write 3–5 sentences about your experience.   ▶ Digital help

   (I didn't like it at first because I wanted to text my friends. But I did lots of fun things instead and had a lot of time for my dog. I slept well afterwards.)

---

[1] **digital detox** *die digitale Entgiftung, das digitale Fasten*   [2] **device** *das Gerät*

7   READING   **Priya's phone call**

▶ SB, p. 112

a)   Priya's grandmother has called her to ask for help. Put the phone conversation in order.

3	Sure, what's the problem?
7	Yes, that's better. What did you say?
12	Bye, <u>Priya</u>!
10	Oh great, thank you!
6	Oh sorry, can you hear me now?
4	Well, it's this new phone. I can't *(crrr)*
2	I'm OK, thank you, <u>Priya</u> – but I need your help!
8	I said I've got a new phone and I don't know how to <u>connect it to the Wi-Fi at home</u>.
11	You're welcome. I have to go now because <u>dinner's ready</u>. See you <u>tomorrow</u>, <u>Grandma</u>!
1	Hi <u>Grandma</u>, nice to hear from you. How are things?
5	Huh? Sorry I can't hear you, <u>Grandma</u>. You're breaking up. Can you say that again, please?
9	No problem, I can come over <u>after school tomorrow</u> and show you.

b)   LISTENING   **Listen and check.**

16

c)   **Answer the questions.**

1   What does Priya's grandmother need help with? *She wants to connect her new phone to the Wi-Fi at home.*

2   When is Priya going to help her? *Priya is going to help her tomorrow after school.*

d)   **Write instructions to help Priya's grandmother. Use the pictures to help you.**

▶ More help, p. 79

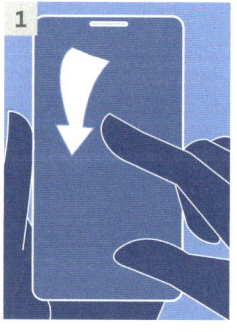

| 1 | 2 | 3 | 4 |
| *Swipe the screen.* | *Tap the Wi-Fi icon, then the Wi-Fi name.* | *Type the password.* | *Connect to the Wi-Fi.* |

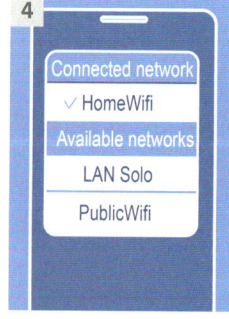

e)   SPEAKING   **Work with a partner. Change the <u>underlined</u> phrases in the dialogue to make a new one, with different people and a new problem. Then act out the dialogue with your partner.**

8 SPEAKING New device

▶ SB, p. 113

a) You and your partner have different instructions for a new device, but you can't read some parts.
Partner B: Look at page 91.
Partner A: Take turns to explain the instructions you can see and complete your copy.

1	Charge the device. _____ _____ _____	4	Tap 'search' on your phone.
2	Switch on the device.	5	Press the Bluetooth button on the device. _____
3	Tap the Bluetooth icon on your phone. _____	6	Tap 'pair' on your phone.
		7	Play music on your phone and listen to it.

b) Look at all the instructions. What device do you think they are for?

(headphones / earpods / airbuds / a bluetooth speaker) _____

9 WRITING Technology

▶ SB, p. 113

a) How confident are you with technology? Give examples.

(I'm very confident with technology because I use my phone and laptop all the
time. I'm learning to code at the moment. / ...) _____

b) Write about a time you asked for help or helped someone with technology.

(Last week, I helped my dad set up his new laptop. And then I asked him for
help because I didn't know how to use the washing machine. / ...) _____

▶ Challenge 1, p. 79

I can **give simple instructions.**

10 READING **Good and bad**

► SB, p. 114

a) Read the three comments in the school magazine about social media and decide if each question is about Kali, Aled or JJ.

www. Llandudno-school.example.com/magazine

Kali

I used to be addicted to¹ social media – I couldn't even eat a sandwich without posting a photo of it online! At first, it felt great getting so many likes and comments, but it began to take over my life. And then I found it was a problem for my well-being too, because if I uploaded a video that wasn't so popular, it made me feel really bad. In the end, I closed all my social media accounts and now I feel a lot happier.

Aled

Sure, like most people, I use a few different social media apps and I think it's a great way to make friends and keep in touch with people. It's not true that social media stops you from seeing people in real life – in fact, I send messages online to help me organize going out with friends! Plus I have family in other countries, so it's nice to share photos and videos with them. Yes, I use social media every day, but I don't think it's a problem.

JJ

I'm fine with social media. It's not my whole life or anything, but I subscribe to a few video channels and I watch them maybe three times a week. I don't upload my own videos because I'm worried about staying private online, but I like following influencers because you can learn a lot. You have to be careful and you can't just believe everything you see, but I think there's more good than bad online.

1 Who uses social media the most? *Aled*

2 Who is worried about putting their private life online? *JJ*

3 Who thinks people say untrue things about social media? *Aled*

4 Who used social media a lot more in the past? *Kali*

5 Who talks about how social media can have an effect on your feelings? *Kali*

6 Who likes watching videos online? *JJ*

b) Highlight the arguments for social media and underline the arguments against social media above.

c) Which of the arguments in b) do you agree most with and why?

(I agree that social media is helpful for organizing meeting friends. / I agree that social media is a problem because it can make you feel bad. / ...)

¹ **addicted to** *süchtig nach*

11 Social media phrases

▶ SB, p. 114

The letters in the words for things you can do on social media are in the wrong order.
Write them correctly.

1   IWTER MECTONSM   *write comments*

2   LOLUWNOF NSOOMEE   *unfollow someone*

3   LAUPOD EDOVSI   *upload videos*

4   RADFORW A KILN   *forward a link*

5   STOP SOPOHT   *post photos*

▶ Challenge 2, p. 80

12 LISTENING Fact or opinion?

17

▶ SB, p. 116

Listen to the voice note from Barri to his little sister and tick (✓) the correct answer.

1   Barri is leaving a voice note because …

☐ he will be home early.   ☐ he wants to join a social network.

✓ his sister shared something online.   ☐ he can't connect to the internet.

2   The post was about …

✓ school life.   ☐ sharing posts at school.

☐ statistics about schools.   ☐ the school's social media account.

3   He talks about a post that …

☐ has lots of facts in it.   ✓ only has opinions in it.

☐ was from an official website.   ☐ was from a newspaper.

4   Barri thinks …

☐ there were too many statistics in the post.   ☐ his sister doesn't want to see her friends.

☐ the things in the post were true.   ✓ people should be careful about what they share.

5   Barri wants his sister to …

☐ come home.   ✓ delete the post.

☐ write a better post.   ☐ be more emotional.

▶ Early finisher 2, p. 78

Erklär-film

13 LANGUAGE **Who or what are they?**   ▶ SB, p. 117

a) Read the sentences and complete them with *who*, *that* or *which*.

1 Dafydd is a man **who/that** is sixty years old.

5 Catrin is a girl **who/that** loves reading.

2 Ceri is a woman **who/that** codes websites.

6 Rhys is a boy **who/that** wears glasses.

3 Bethan is a robot **which/that** answers questions.

7 Ffion is a robot **which/that** is very clever.

4 Elen is a robot **which/that** looks like a dog.

8 Bryn is a robot **which/that** repairs things.

b) Match the names from a) with the correct people and robots.

A

Rhys

B

Dafydd

C

Bryn

D

Catrin

E

Ffion

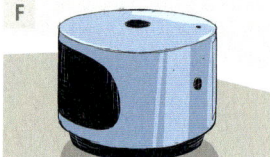

F

Bethan

G

Elen

H

Ceri

14 LANGUAGE **Guess who or what**   ▶ SB, p. 117

a) Think of a person, an animal and a thing. Then write definitions using *who*, *that* or *which*.

1 **(Frau Schmidt)** is a person **(who teaches our English class)** .

2 **(An elephant)** is an animal **(that is very big)** .

3 **(A book)** is something **(which you can read)** .

b) SPEAKING Describe the person, animal and thing from a) to your partner. Your partner guesses what they are, then swap roles.

> *I'm thinking of a person / an animal / something … who/which/that …*

c) Find three new words from this unit and write a definition of them using *who*, *that* or *which*.

(A watch is a thing that tells you the time.)

(A cardigan is something that you wear to keep warm.)

(A gymnast is someone who does gymnastics.)

I can talk about the good and bad sides of social media. ✓

15 READING **Who's thinking that?**

► SB, pp. 118–120

Read the story on pages 118–119 in your book and decide whether Dylan, Owen or Saskia thinks each sentence.

1 'I don't understand why Dylan wrote that – it's not true!' _Owen_

2 'Wow, I'm becoming really popular online!' _Dylan_

3 'I hope Saskia thinks I look good in this photo.' _Dylan_

4 'This is strange. He's not what I expected.' _Saskia_

5 'Ha, if people laugh at him, they'll know he lied before!' _Owen_

⊠ 16 **Good and bad choices**

► More help, p. 80   ► SB, pp. 118–120

What good and bad choices did Dylan and Owen make in the story? Make notes in the table.

	good choices	bad choices
Dylan	– helped Owen with social media	– put things that weren't true on social media
	– stopped worrying about how he looked online	– only cared about how he looked
Owen	– said sorry	– posted a mean photo of Dylan without asking

17 WRITING **Before and after**

► Digital help 🔁   ► SB, pp. 118–120

a) Look at these photos of an influencer. Write what's different in the two photos, which things she has used to change the photos. Write about hair, make-up, position, lighting and filters.

(The influencer has changed her hair because it's straight in the first photo, but it's styled in the second. She is wearing more make-up and is standing/sitting in a different position. I think she has used a filter because her skin looks too perfect.)

b) What do you think about the second picture? Do you like it or not? Say why.

(I like the second picture, she worked hard to edit it and she looks good. / I don't like the second picture because it doesn't look like her anymore and it's not real.)

18 Opposites

Write the opposites of these words from the unit.

1 follow ↔ _unfollow_

2 with ↔ _without_

3 positive ↔ _negative_

4 lose touch ↔ _keep in touch_

5 his ↔ _hers_

6 disagree ↔ _agree_

7 international ↔ _national_

8 public ↔ _private_

19 Definitions

Read the definitions and add the missing words.

1 _Rugby_ is a game that lots of people in Wales like to play.

2 _Coal mining_ is an industry which was very important to Wales in the past.

3 An _instrument_ is something that you can play to make music.

4 A _screenshot_ is a picture that shows what's on your screen.

20 Technology words

a) Many technology words are the same in different languages. Highlight the words that are similar in German.

charger, computer, device, document, headphones, internet, keyboard, laptop, network, screen, voice-over, website

b) Can you think of technology words in other languages that are similiar in English?

(вéб-сáйт, кóмп'ютéр, інтéрфéйс, Інтéрнéт, скáнéр, …)

21 SPEAKING Speak English well: the letter W

🔊 18 a) Listen and repeat the words. Which word doesn't have a W sound? Cross it out (~~cross out~~).

1 Wales   2 Wi-Fi   3 walk   4 watch

5 which   6 ~~who~~   7 when   8 worry

b) Look at yourself in a mirror when you say the words.
Tick (✓) the correct mouth shape for a W sound in English.

 ✓    ☐

🔊 19 c) Listen and repeat the tongue twister. Focus on the W sounds.

Why would we walk to Wales when we can watch wonderful waterfalls in the wild?

In Unit 4, I was most interested in learning about *(social media / Wales / ...)*

because *(I want to be an influencer. / I've never visited Wales. / ...)*

My progress[1]

Write an adjective to describe how you found each of the *I can* statements.
You can use ideas from the box or your own ideas.

boring • difficult • easy • (not) important • interesting • scary • useful

Remember: everything is difficult before it becomes easy!

1 I can understand information about Wales: I found this *(easy. / ...)*

2 I can talk about Wales: I found this *(a bit boring. / ...)*

3 I can give simple instructions: I found this *(difficult. / ...)*

4 I can talk about the good and bad sides of social media: I found this *(interesting. / ...)*

5 I can talk about truth and lies on social media: I found this *(important. / ...)*

6 I can make a talk flow: I found this *(quite difficult. / ...)*

7 I can give a short talk about social media: I found this *(scary. / ...)*

Thinking about how I improved

Look back at your learner log for Unit 3 on page 61. Which things did you do to improve? Which were the most helpful and why?

I used ... to practise.	I asked ... for help.	I practised ... with ...
I tried ...	I read/listened ...	It was / wasn't helpful because ...

(I practised the new vocabulary with my brother. It was helpful because he corrected my pronunciation and gave me tips. I tried reading a book in English, but it wasn't helpful because it was too difficult.)

---

[1] **progress** *der Fortschritt*

Early finisher 1 **Welsh facts**

Read the facts about Wales and guess which four are true.
Use the letters of the correct answers to spell out something you can find in Llandudno.

P	I	E	R

T	There are more cows than people in Wales.
R	Wales has a place called Fairy Glen, and many people believe fairies live there.
N	Wales has more vegetarians than the rest of the UK.
P	Wales has more castles per square mile than any other European country.
A	Wales has the highest mountain in the UK.
E	Mount Everest is named after a Welsh man who made the first map of the mountain.
S	Welsh doesn't use the letter E.
I	St Davids in Wales is the UK's smallest city, with fewer than 2,000 people.

► Check

Early finisher 2 **Break the code**

a) Dylan has used an app to put some words into code. Break the code and write the words!

#	%	*	]	◇	⌐	≠	{	=	>	≤	≈	}
a	b	c	d	e	f	g	h	i	j	k	l	m
△	<	≥	@	∟	§	£	□	±	+	‼	♪	[
n	o	p	q	r	s	t	u	v	w	x	y	z

1 =△§£#≈≈   install

2 §+=≥◇   swipe

3 *<△△◇*£   connect

4 *{#∟≠◇   charge

5 ≥∟◇§§   press

6 £#≥   tap

b) Write a message to your partner in Dylan's code. Can your partner decode it?

({◇≈≈<, {<+ =§ =£ ≠<=△≠?   Hello, how is it going?)

► Check

7 [More help] Priya's phone call
▶ WB, p. 70 ▶ SB, p. 112

d) Write instructions to help Priya's grandmother. Use the words in the box and the pictures to help you.

connect • icon • password • screen • swipe • tap • type

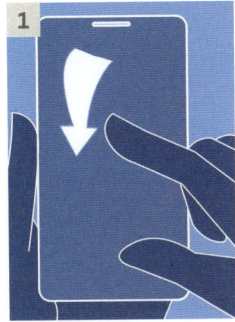

Swipe the
screen.

Tap the Wi-Fi icon, then
the Wi-Fi name.

Type the
password.

Connect to
the Wi-Fi.

[Challenge 1] Then and now
▶ WB, p. 71

Look at the cartoon and answer the questions.

1 What can you see in the picture on the left?
There's *a boy and his dad. The boy is*
asking his dad for help because he
needs batteries for his toy car.

2 What's different in the picture on the right?
The boy *and his dad are older. The boy*
is now a teenager. The dad is asking the teenager for help because he has a
problem with his laptop.

3 What does this say about how things change as we get older?
When we're young, *we need our parents to help us,*

but when we're older, *our parents need us to help them.*

4 What do you ask for help with at home?
(I ask my mum for help with my homework. / ...)

5 What do people at home ask you for help with?
(My stepdad asks me for help with his phone. / ...)
▶ Check

Challenge 2 **A new social media app**   ▶ Digital help 🔖   ▶ WB, p. 73

a)   Work with a partner and design a social media app.

Step 1: What can you do on the app? What do you need it for?

(You can upload photos, videos and songs. You can chat online and write comments. You can discuss homework. / ...)

Step 2: Who can use the app?

(Only people at my school. / in my class. / ...)

Step 5: Draw a logo.

Step 3: What are the rules of the app?

(You can't be mean to people or write horrible comments. You can't post things that aren't true. Don't post the solutions to homework, only discuss it. / ...)

Step 4: Think of a short name for your app.

(SchoolTok)

b)   Present your app to another pair. Then swap roles.

c)   Would you use the other pair's app? Say why or why not.

(I would use their app because it sounds like fun. / is useful. / I wouldn't use their app because I already have an app like that. / I don't need it. / ...)

16 **More help** **Good and bad choices**   ▶ WB, p. 75   ▶ SB, pp. 118–120

What good and bad choices did Dylan and Owen make in the story? Complete the notes in the table.

	good choices	bad choices
Dylan	– helped Owen with *social media*	– put *things that weren't true* on social media
	– stopped worrying about *how he looked online*	– only cared about *how he looked*
Owen	– said *sorry*	– posted *a mean photo of Dylan* without asking

1 Technology words

Write the correct words to label the picture of the devices.

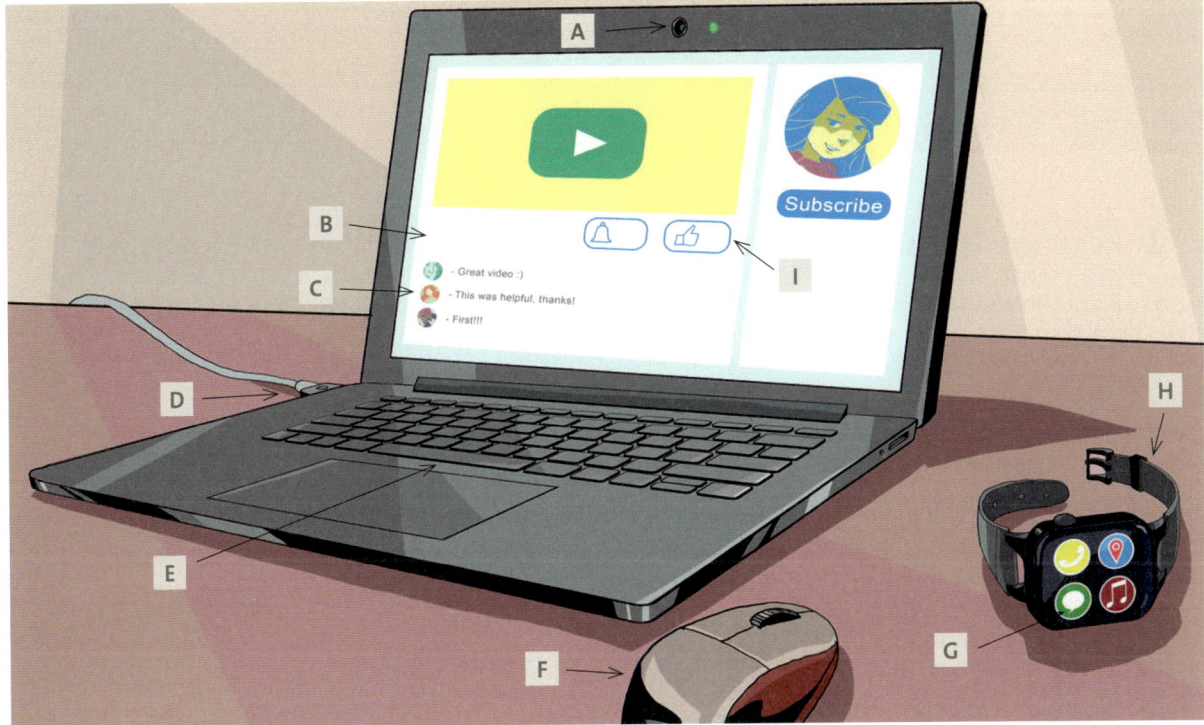

A _camera_   B _screen_   C _comment_

D _charger_   E _keyboard_   F _mouse_

G _app/icon_   H _smartwatch_   I _likes_

2 Dylan's charger

Complete the conversation with the correct possessive pronouns.

Dylan Oh no, my phone is about to die[1], and I left my charger at home. Owen, can I borrow (1) _yours_, please?

Owen Sorry Dylan. I never bring (2) _mine_ to school. Look, there's Louise. Maybe you could use (3) _hers_?

Dylan No, she's got a different kind of charger to (4) _mine_. But I could ask Promit because (5) _his_ is the same, I think. Hey, Promit! Do you have your charger with you? I think (6) _ours_ are the same, right?

Promit Yeah, I do, but the Evans brothers are using it because (7) _theirs_ is broken. Sorry!

Owen Bad luck, Dylan. Looks like you can't use your phone at break, and you'll have to talk to me instead!

▶ Check ⤵

---

[1] (to) **die** sterben

Unit 5
Two Irelands: Together

1 READING The island's top 6

▸ Digital help 🔖   ▸ SB, p.139

a) Read the website and choose the best place for these people to visit. You don't need one place.

1 'I want to try Irish food and learn about Irish history.' *Dublin*

2 'I don't want to go anywhere too busy, and I don't want to drive.' *The Aran Islands*

3 'I want to hear Irish songs and look at beautiful paintings.' *Galway*

4 'I want to visit the coast and I love adventure!' *Carrick-a-Rede Rope Bridge*

5 'I love nature and I want to try surfing.' *Kerry*

Top 6 places to visit in Ireland and Northern Ireland

- **Galway** is a very creative city, full of art galleries and street art. You can hear traditional music every night in one of the many pubs[1].

- **Kerry** has maybe the most beautiful road in the world, the Ring of Kerry. It's a 111-mile-long circle by the coast where you can see mountains, islands and beaches, as well as do water sports or horse riding.

- **Cork** is the second-biggest city in Ireland and has lots of beautiful buildings. Maybe the most famous is the nearby Blarney Castle with the Blarney Stone[2]. Legend says that if you kiss[3] the stone, you will be great at speaking!

- **Dublin** is famous for being a party city with fantastic food and drink. But it also has more than 40 museums.

- **The Aran Islands** are three small islands that still have a traditional way of life. Gaelic is the first language here and you're not allowed to bring your car. Instead, horses pull carts[4] to carry people around.

- **The Carrick-a-Rede Rope Bridge** is a way to walk over to a small island off the coast of Country Antrim – but only if you're brave! It moves a lot in the wind and it's 30 metres above the sea!

b) Which of these places would you most like to visit and why?

I'd like to visit *(Kerry because I love hiking. / ...)*

[1] **pub** *die Kneipe*   [2] **stone** *der Stein*   [3] (to) **kiss** *küssen*   [4] **cart** *der Wagen*

I can **talk about Ireland and Northern Ireland.**

2 MEDIATION **A Derry B&B** ▶ SB, p. 141

a) Your uncle wants to visit Derry in Northern Ireland with your cousin. He has found this advert for a B&B online, but he doesn't understand it. Read the advert and answer his questions in German.

Tara's Place

Right in the busy city centre, Tara's Place is perfect for anyone visiting Derry! We have ten comfortable rooms on both the ground floor and first floor (5 double rooms at £70 a night, and 5 single rooms at £55 a night), all with their own bathroom with a bath and shower. Our beautiful rooms also have a kettle, desk and TV.

There's free Wi-Fi in the dining room only.

A delicious breakfast of toast, cereals and bread with tea or coffee is included in the price. Visit our website now to book!

1   Wie viel kostet ein Zimmer für zwei Personen? *Es kostet £70 pro Nacht.*

2   Wir brauchen ein Zimmer mit zwei Einzelbetten – geht das? *Nein, es gibt keine Zweibettzimmer.*

3   Welche Ausstattung haben die Zimmer? *Jedes Zimmer hat ein eigenes Badezimmer, einen Wasserkocher, Schreibtisch und Fernseher.*

4   Gibt es Zimmer im Erdgeschoss? *Ja, es gibt Zimmer im Erdgeschoss.*

5   Ich muss an einer Online-Konferenz im Zimmer teilnehmen. Gibt es WLAN? *Ja, aber nicht im Zimmer, sondern nur im Essbereich.*

6   Was gibt es zum Frühstück? Ich möchte ein typisch englisches Frühstück. *Es gibt nur Toast, Frühstücksflocken und Brot sowie Tee oder Kaffee.*

7   Wie kann ich ein Zimmer reservieren? *Man kann auf der Webseite reservieren.*

b) Do you think *Tara's Place* is a good B&B for your uncle and cousin? Why or why not?
No, because there's no Wi-Fi in the room and no English breakfast. There are no twin rooms.

▶ Challenge 1, p. 89

3 LISTENING A special tour of Belfast

▶ SB, p. 143

🔊 20

a) **Listen to the tour guide and say if each sentence is true (T) or false (F).**

1 This is a walking tour.   F

2 The tour starts in a Catholic neighbourhood.   T

3 The Belfast murals are all from the same time. F

4 The Peace Walls were built to celebrate peace in Northern Ireland.   F

5 The tour guide remembers when the city was divided.   T

6 The next place on the tour is a museum. T

b) **Listen again and correct the false sentences from a).**

1 This is a tour in a taxi.

3 The Belfast murals are from different times / from the 90s and more recently.

4 The Peace Walls were built to stop people moving from one neighbourhood to another.

4 READING Visiting the market

▶ SB, p. 143

Read Orla's message to her friend and choose the correct word for each gap.

> clothes • funny • morning • musicians • sausage • stall • world

Hey Siân! Mum, Jack and I went to St George's market this

(1) _morning_ before we flew home from Belfast. It was so cool!

There were 200 stalls selling everything you can think of: food,

(2) _clothes_ , gifts, art, everything! I bought a

(3) _funny_ T-shirt to take home, so I can remember this

amazing trip. You can find food from all round the (4) _world_

at the market, but Jack showed us his favourite food (5) _stall_ and we got a special snack

called the Belfast Bap – it's a bread roll[1] with (6) _sausage_ , bacon and egg, and it was SO good!

We sat and watched some (7) _musicians_ playing the guitar while we ate. I didn't want to leave! I

want to visit Belfast again soon.

Belfast Bap

▶ Early finisher 1, p. 88

[1] **bread roll** das Brötchen

I can **talk and write about Belfast.**

5 READING Who was it?
▶ SB, pp. 144–146

Read the story on pages 144–145 and choose the correct character for each question: Declan, Jack, Quinn or Orla.

1   Who had a nice afternoon with Jack? *Orla*

2   Who was bullied because of their hobby? *Jack*

3   Who says Jack will win the competition? *Quinn*

4   Who thinks it's important that a dancer from Northern Ireland is the winner? *Declan*

5   Who was the last person to dance? *Orla*

6 Feelings
▶ SB, pp. 144–146

a) How did Orla feel at these points in the story? You can write more than one feeling.

When Orla thought about her afternoon with Jack, she felt *happy.*

When Orla saw Jack in the competition, she felt *surprised.*

Before Orla went up to dance the first time, she felt *confident.*

Before Orla's second dance, she felt *nervous.*

When Orla made a mistake, she felt *angry / worried.*

b) How would you feel if you danced in a competition, and why?

I would feel *(nervous because I don't like being on a stage. / confident because I'm good at dancing. / …)*

7 Bringing the two Irelands together
▶ More help, p. 89   ▶ SB, pp. 144–146

a) WRITING The aim of the dance competition was to bring young people from Ireland and Northern Ireland together and to help keep peace. Do you think this was a good idea? Why or why not?

(Yes, because they could meet people from the other country. / No, because some people only wanted to win and were mean. / …)

b) What other activities could bring young people from the two countries together? Write your own ideas.

(football match / party / camp / …)

I can **complete a story.** ✓

8 A–Z

a) Try to find a travel word for as many letters as you can. Then compare with your partner.

A	*accommodation, (airport, ...)*	**M**	*(map, market, ...)*
B	*(B&B, bus, ...)*	**N**	*(nature, north, ...)*
C	*(cab, campsite, ...)*	**O**	*(one way, order, ...)*
D	*(desk, double bed, ...)*	**P**	*(palace, passport, ...)*
E	*(east, email, ...)*	**Q**	*(question, queue, ...)*
F	*(ferry, food, ...)*	**R**	*(reservation, room, ...)*
G	*(guest, go, ...)*	**S**	*(sight, shower, ...)*
H	*(helicopter, hotel, ...)*	**T**	*(tent, train, ...)*
I	*(ID card, Ireland, ...)*	**U**	*(UK, underground, ...)*
J	*(journey, jungle, ...)*	**V**	*(visit, vlog, ...)*
K	*(kettle, key, ...)*	**W**	*(wardrobe, Wi-Fi, ...)*
L	*(lake, lift, ...)*	**X/Y/Z**	*(youth hostel, zoo, ...)*

b) Choose three words from a) and write a sentence to explain what they mean. Then swap with a partner and guess the word.

1 *(a place where you can stay in a tent on holiday: campsite)*

2 *(something in a hotel room that you use to make tea or coffee: kettle)*

3 *(someone who stays in a hotel or at your house: guest)*

9 SPEAKING Speak English well: questions

a) Listen to the questions. Which go up at the end (↑) and which go down at the end (↓)?

21

1 Do you have a reservation? ↑   2 How much is a double room? ↓

3 Where are the Peace Walls? ↓   4 Have you been to Belfast before? ↑

5 Who is the manager of this hotel? ↓   6 Did you have a good journey? ↑

b) Look at your answers for a) and complete the sentence.

Yes/No-questions go *up* _____ at the end and wh-questions go *down* _____ at the end.

In Unit 5, I was most interested in learning about *(Belfast / the Troubles / ...)*

_____

because *(I want to visit Ireland. / I'm interested in history. / ...)*

_____

My progress[1]

Complete the sentences to say how confident you are about the *I can* statements.

the easiest • quite easy • a bit difficult • the most difficult

💡 Aim for the moon, even if you land in the stars.

I can talk about Ireland and Northern Ireland. This is *(quite easy / ...)* _____ for me.

I can plan and talk about a trip. This is *(the easiest / ...)* _____ for me.

I can talk and write about Belfast. This is *(a bit difficult / ...)* _____ for me.

I can complete a story. This is *(the most difficult / ...)* for me.

Looking back at this year

Look at your learner logs for all the units this year and complete the sentences.

My favourite unit was *(unit 1 / ...)* _____ because *(I think London is a really cool city. / ...)* _____

The easiest topic for me was *(technology / ...)* _____

because *(a lot of the words are the same in German. / ...)* _____

The most difficult topic for me was *(the Troubles / ...)* _____

because *(it was difficult to understand and I don't like history. / ...)* _____

I want to find out more about *(places in Scotland. / ...)* _____

Next year, to improve my English, I will *(use digital help more. / listen to podcasts in English. / play my video game in English. /...)* _____

_____

[1] **progress** *der Fortschritt*

Early finisher 1 WRITING **A dream trip to Dublin**

Read all the information and choose transport, accommodation and activities for your dream trip to Dublin. You can spend €350.

Return flights
Two hours
€150

Return train and ferry
Nine hours
€80

Return coach and ferry
Fifteen hours
€50

Central Youth Hostel
A small family room with a shared bathroom. No TV or Wi-Fi.
€40 a night

Paddy's B&B
A comfortable family room with private bathroom and free breakfast.
€70 a night

Hotel De Luxe
A beautiful family room with private bathroom, TV with games console, fast Wi-Fi and delicious breakfast.
€100 a night

Dublin Castle
Visit this historical castle and its beautiful gardens, plus get a beautiful view of the city from the top of the tower.
€4

Dublin Zoo
See all your favourite animals, including elephants, penguins and lions in the centre of a big park.
€20

George's Street Arcade
An indoor market with independent shops and food stalls.
free (except for what you buy!)

Bus tour
A bus tour of Dublin, which will take you around all the main sights of the city. You can get on and off the bus to visit different places.
€28

Forty Foot
A local secret, this is a big cliff at the beach that is perfect for jumping into the sea and swimming – if you're brave enough to face the cold water!
free

National Leprechaun Museum
A fun museum all about the magic and legends of Ireland. You can take lots of funny photos here too!
€12

I'm going to travel by (train and ferry / ...) _____ because (I like train rides / ...)

_____ and stay for (two / ...) _____ nights at

(the Central Youth Hostel / ...) _____ because (it's the cheapest. / ...)

I'm going to visit (the National Leprechaun Museum / ...) _____ and

(do a bus tour / ...) _____ because (I want to see all the sights of Dublin. / ...)

I will spend the rest of my money on (shopping at George's Street Arcade. / ...)

But I'm not going to (visit Dublin Zoo / ...) _____ because (I don't like

zoos. / ...) _____ ▶ Check

Challenge 1 READING **Which room?** ▶ WB, p. 83

Read the sentences and decide who should stay in which room in the B&B.

1 Mr & Mrs Chen need a room on the ground floor because Mr Chen uses a wheelchair.

2 Mrs Attal and her wife need a double room with a small bed and a bath for their baby.

3 Miss Connelly is travelling with her two sons, and they all need their own bed.

4 Mr Murphy needs somewhere to work in his room as he is on a business trip.

5 Mr Codona and his son would like a bath, not a shower.

6 Mr & Mrs Doherty and their daughter don't want to be on the ground floor because it's too loud.

D
A
F
B
E
C

▶ Check

---

7 **More help** **Bringing the two Irelands together**   ▶ WB, p. 85   ▶ SB, pp. 144–146

a) The aim of dance competition was to bring young people from Ireland and Northern Ireland together to help keep peace. Do you think this was a good idea? Why or why not?

I think/don't think it was a good idea because	the dancers some dancers it's a good way to	meet people from the other country. / of a different religion. / who were different. test their skills. build their confidence. make friends.
		make no friends. be against each other.

Unit 1 **Topic 3 | Exercise 13** ▶ WB, p. 26 ▶ SB, p. 24

Partner B: Ask your partner for the missing information and complete your menu.

> How much is ...?

> What costs £ ...?

> What's in a ...?

Greg's Breakfast Cafe

Big English breakfast (bacon[1], *eggs*, sausage, mushrooms[2], *baked beans*)	£7.50	Turkish breakfast (bread, hummus, olives, eggs, tomatoes)	*£6.50*
Vegetarian English breakfast (eggs, mushrooms, tomatoes, baked beans)	*£6.25*	Muesli with *milk* or yoghurt	£2.25
		Fruit salad	£2.75
Eggs on toast	£3.50	Tea or coffee	*£1.75*
Pancakes	£3.25	Fruit juice	£1.50
Toast with *butter* and jam	£2.00	Sparkling *water*	£1.50

Unit 2 **Topic 3 | Exercise 14** ▶ WB, p. 42 ▶ SB, p. 55

a) Partner B: Read the advert on the right and answer your partner's questions.

b) Ask your partner these questions and write the answers.

1 What's the advert for? *It's for a confidence app.*

CONFIDENCE CLUB

All students are welcome to come and help their confidence through different exercises. Come along to **CONFIDENCE CLUB** and you'll learn to act, dance and talk in public – and hopefully to **BELIEVE IN YOURSELF TOO!**

We meet every Thursday at lunchtime in room 7. Speak to **MRS GIBSON** to sign up!

2 How can it help people be more confident?
There are games, exercises and videos with tips and compliments to make you feel more positive.

3 When can people do this? *They can always use the app.*

4 How much does it cost? *Nothing, it's a free app.*

c) Which activity do you think is best and why? Write the answer and compare with your partner.
(I like the app best because you can use it any time. / I don't like acting. / I like the 'confidence club' best because you can make friends. / I like dancing. / ...)

---

[1] **bacon** *der Speck*   [2] **mushroom** *der Pilz*

Unit 3 **Topic 2 | Exercise 7** ▶ WB, p. 54 ▶ SB, p. 80

a) Partner B: Ask your partner for the missing information and answer their questions.

> *What can you do on (day) at (time) …?*

> *How much does … cost?*

	9 o'clock		12 o'clock		3 o'clock	
Monday	paddle boarding	£10	*skiing*	£30	swimming	*£5*
Tuesday	*snowboarding*	£30	*kayaking*	£15	mountain biking	*£25*
Wednesday	cliff jumping	£20	mountain biking	*£25*	*snowboarding*	£30
Thursday	swimming	*£5*	paddle boarding	£10	cliff jumping	£20
Friday	*kayaking*	£15	swimming	*£5*	*skiing*	£30

b) Decide with your partner which three activities you would both like to do. When are they and how much will it cost in total?

Unit 4 **Topic 2 | Exercise 8** ▶ WB, p. 71 ▶ SB, p. 113

a) Partner B: Take turns to explain the instructions you can see and complete your copy.

1   *Charge the device.* _____ _____

5   *Press the _____ Bluetooth button on the device.*

2   *Switch on the _____ device.* _____

6   *Tap 'pair' on your phone.* _____

3   *Tap the Bluetooth icon on your phone.*

7   *Play music on your phone and listen to it.*

4   *Tap 'search' on your phone.* _____

b) Look at all the instructions. What device do you think they are for?

(headphones / earpods / airbuds / a bluetooth speaker)

Typical tasks

Typical tasks	Häufige Arbeitsanweisungen
Act out the conversation / scene.	Führt das Gespräch / die Szene vor.
Answer the questions / partner B's questions.	Beantworte die Fragen / Partner/in Bs Fragen.
Ask questions.	Stelle Fragen.
Check with your partner.	Überprüfe mit deiner Partnerin / deinem Partner.
Choose the correct verbs / a person / ...	Wähle die richtigen Verben / eine Person / ...
Circle the correct word / correct verb / ...	Kreise das richtige Wort / das richtige Verb / ... ein.
Compare the pictures / your answers / ... with a partner.	Vergleiche die Bilder / deine Antworten / ... mit einem/r Partner/in.
Complete the questions / table / ...	Vervollständige die Fragen / Tabelle / ...
Correct the false / wrong sentences / answers.	Berichtige die falschen Sätze / Antworten.
Cross out (cross out) the numbers / wrong things / ...	Streiche die Nummern / die falschen Dinge / ... durch.
Describe the picture.	Beschreibe das Bild.
Draw pictures / lines / ...	Zeichne / Male Bilder / Linien / ...
Explain why.	Begründe (deine Antwort).
Fill the gaps with the correct words.	Vervollständige die Lücken mit den richtigen Wörtern.
Find the answers / correct picture / ...	Finde die Antworten / das richtige Bild / ...
Give reasons.	Begründe (deine Antwort).
Highlight the letters / words / ...	Markiere die Buchstaben / Wörter / ...
Listen again.	Höre nochmal zu.
Listen and check / read / write / ...	Höre zu und überprüfe / lies / schreibe / ...
Listen to the words / sentences / people / ...	Höre dir die Wörter / Sätze / Leute / ... an.
Look at the picture / answers / ...	Schau dir das Bild / die Antworten / ... an.
Match the pictures / ... with the sentences / ...	Ordne die Bilder / ... den Sätzen / ... zu.
Practise with a partner.	Übt zu zweit.
Put a cross (✗) in the box for the wrong sentences.	Setze ein Kreuzchen ins Kästchen für die falschen Sätze.
Put a tick (✓) in the box for the correct sentences / in the correct boxes.	Setze ein Häkchen ins Kästchen für die richtigen Sätze / in die richtigen Kästchen.
Put the words in the correct order.	Bringe die Wörter in die richtige Reihenfolge.
Read about ...	Lies über ...
Read the messages / sentences / text / ...	Lies die Nachrichten / Sätze / den Text / ...
Right (✓) or wrong (✗)? / True (T) or false (F)?	Richtig oder falsch?
Swap roles.	Wechselt die Rollen.
Take turns.	Wechselt euch ab.
Talk to a partner.	Sprich mit einem/r Partner/in.
Tick (✓) the correct definition / the hobbies / ...	Hake alle richtigen Definitionen / Hobbys / ... ab.
Underline ...	Unterstreiche ...
Use the words / sentences / ... to help you.	Benutze die Wörter / Sätze / ... als Hilfe.
Use words from the box.	Benutze die Wörter aus dem Kasten.
Watch part 1 / 2 / ... (again).	Sieh dir Teil 1 / 2 / ... (nochmal) an.
Work with a partner.	Arbeitet zu zweit.
Write about six sports / your grandma / ...	Schreibe über sechs Sportarten / deine Oma / ...
Write the correct definitions / answers / sentences / ...	Schreibe die richtigen Definitionen / Antworten / Sätze / ...